TWAYNE'S WORLD AUTHORS SERIES

A Survey of the World's Literature

Sylvia E. Bowman, Indiana University

GENERAL EDITOR

Australia

Joseph Jones, University of Texas

Editor

Adam Lindsay Gordon

(TWAS 41)

TWAYNE'S WORLD AUTHORS SERIES (TWAS)

The purpose of TWAS is to survey the major writers —novelists, dramatists, historians, poets, philosophers, and critics—of the nations of the world. Among the national literatures covered are those of Australia, Canada, China, Eastern Europe, France, Germany, Greece, India, Italy, Japan, Latin America, New Zealand, Poland, Russia, Scandinavia, Spain, and the African nations, as well as Hebrew, Yiddish, and Latin Classical literatures. This survey is complemented by Twayne's United States Authors Series and English Authors Series.

The intent of each volume in these series is to present a critical analytical study of the works of the writer; to include biographical and historical material that may be necessary for understanding, appreciation, and critical appraisal of the writer; and to present all material in clear, concise English—but not to vitiate the scholarly content of the work by doing so.

Adam Lindsay Gordon

By C. F. MacRae

Twayne Publishers, Inc.　：：　New York

Library of Congress Catalog Card Number: 68-20812

Manufactured in the United States of America

Preface

THIS book about Adam Lindsay Gordon's poetry is not a "life," or even a "life and letters," of the poet. That is a task more fitting for the biographer than for the student of literature. Besides, Gordon's poetry is singularly unrelated to the sequence of events in his life. Whereas the life of Browning, for example, was marked by the succession of his published works, from *Pauline* to *Asolando,* Gordon's publications came in a bunch in his final years. Although many of his poems are derived from his experience and most of them are visibly rooted in his character and temperament, there is little significant "development" in his literary production. It is true that his worst poetry appears in his first volume and his most popular poems in the third and last; nevertheless, the most quoted lines are to be found in the second volume published almost simultaneously with the first.

To try to use the events of Gordon's life as a framework for a discussion of his poetry would result in a serious imbalance. Therefore an introductory biographical outline has been placed at the beginning, as Chapter 1, including two supplementary sections on his character and on the facts of his successive publications. The remaining chapters attempt to deal directly with the poetry itself.

The chief purpose of this volume has been neither to praise nor to dispraise. We have seen too much of both over the years since Gordon's death nearly a century ago. The present aim has been simply to examine Gordon's poetry, to see what it is, and how it is, and as far as possible why it is. If there is an ulterior motive, it is to persuade the reader to take Gordon's poetry—or "verse" if he prefers the term—seriously and to read it for what he may get from it, with a minimum of bias, either nationalistic or narrowly aesthetic.

Acknowledgments must be kept to a minimum, lest omission by inadvertence prove invidious. I should like first of all to mention the late Professor A. S. P. Woodhouse, of the University of Toronto, for many forms of help and encouragement given in times past, and specifically for having first turned my attention to the literature of the British Commonwealth. Thanks are due to the staffs of the Mitchell Library in Sydney, the Public Library in Melbourne, the South Australian Archives in Adelaide, and the Australian National Library in Canberra, for their ready assistance. Lastly, I should like to mention four of those who especially helped to make my brief stay in Australia both pleasant and fruitful. These were Mr. Hugh McCredie, the Deputy Registrar of the University of Sydney; Mr. Neil Burgess, of the University of New South Wales; Professor H. K. H. Hunt, of the University of Melbourne; and Professor T. Inglis Moore, of the Australian National University. To fail to mention their respective wives, "by the name of most kind hostesses," would be not only ungracious but unjust.

University of Waterloo, Ontario   C. F. MACRAE

Contents

Contents

Chronology

1833   Adam Lindsay Gordon born, at Horta in the Azores.

1840   The Gordons settle at Cheltenham.

1841- Attends Cheltenham College.
1842

1848- Attends Royal Military Academy, Woolwich.
1851

1852   Attends Royal Worcester Grammar School.

1853   Leaves England, on August 7.
       November 14-24, arrives at Adelaide, applies to, and is
       accepted by, the South Australian Mounted Police.

1853- Stationed at Mount Gambier and Penola.
1855

1855   Resigns from Mounted Police. Becomes an intinerant
       horse-breaker.

1857   Meets the Rev. J. Tenison Woods.

1861   Receives legacy from mother's estate, of £7000.

1862   Marries Margaret Park, October 20.

1864   Purchases Dingley Dell, March 8.
       The Feud published, August 30.

1865   Elected to South Australian Parliament, March 1.

1866   Resigns his seat in parliament, November 20.
       Lands in Western Australia, December 11.

1867   Returns from Western Australia in March.
       Ashtaroth published, June 10.
       Sea Spray and Smoke Drift published, June 19.
       Takes lease of Craig's Livery stable, in November.

1868   Gives up the livery stable, and leaves Ballarat, October 1.
       Spends two months with Robert Power.

1869   Takes lodgings at 10, Lewis Street, Brighton, March 27.
       Takes steps to make his claim to Esslemont, December.

1870   Continues living at Brighton.
       Bush Ballads and Galloping Rhymes published, June 23.
       Dies, June 24.
       Gravestone erected in Brighton Cemetery, October.

1887   Obelisk erected at Blue Lake, Mount Gambier.

1910   First regular pilgrimage to Brighton Cemetery, September 11. Gordon Memorial Committee formed.

1922   South Australian government purchases Dingley Dell.

1932   Gordon statue unveiled in Spring Street, Melbourne, October 29.

1934   Gordon bust unveiled in the Poets' Corner of Westminster Abbey, May 11.

CHAPTER 1

The Life

A DAM Lindsay Gordon's life was a tragedy in the classical pattern. There was a rising action, a turning point, and a falling action. There was fortuitous prosperity followed by a fateful and irresistible decline toward destitution; there was *hamartia*; there was the futile, half-hearted struggle (half-hearted because sensed as futile) against inexorable destiny; there were repeated blows of misfortune, physical, financial, and emotional; there was even a post-mortem apotheosis which reached a climax sixty-three years after his death. And there were five acts to the drama.

Act One, the exposition, has to do with Gordon's ancestry and birth, his schooling and adolescence, and his exile to Australia. Act Two, the rising action, shows him as a Mounted Policeman and hired horse-breaker, not rich or famous nor likely to become so, but reasonably happy, living a life which he felt suited him and becoming acclimatized in mind and body to the country which had become his home. In Act Three, the central climax, he acquired a wife, a fortune, a settled abode, and the prestige of a legislator and a public figure. Then came the falling action, Act Four, in which he lost all except the wife and a useless residuum of the prestige. Difficulties thickened about him. Discouragement dogged his thoughts. Yet there appeared for a time one dazzling hope of security and competence, not for himself (because he believed that he was near his end, no matter what happened) but for his wife. Act Five, the denouement, snuffed out the hope and his life.

I Youth in England

There is said to be a proverb once current among the farmers of Vermont: "When you're born, you're done for." Lindsay Gordon was done for nine months before he was born. His heredity was his initial misfortune.

9

The marriage of first cousins is not necessarily bad, but if there is any weakness in the common heredity, there is an obvious risk that the marriage of cousins may intensify it. Lindsay's father and mother were both Gordons, and in both (latent in one, active in the other) were the twin strains of wildness and morbidity that marked another and more famous Gordon line, that of "Mad Jack" Gordon and his grandson, Lord Byron. Both of Adam Lindsay Gordon's grandfathers were sons of Robert Gordon of Hallhead and of Lady Henrietta Gordon. Lady Henrietta's parents, too, were both of the Gordon line. Her grandfathers were George Gordon, the first Earl of Aberdeen (1637-1728) and Alexander Gordon, the second Duke of Gordon (1637-1728). In a word, Lindsay had too much Gordon blood in him, and the phrase "gay Gordons" has an ironical as well as a more literal significance.

The poet's father, Adam Durnford Gordon, was a retired captain of the Bengal Cavalry, who had been invalided home before the age of thirty. In 1829 he married his cousin, Harriet Gordon, an heiress with £20,000 safely invested at three-and-a-half per cent. Captain Gordon's relations with his son appear to have been fairly good under continued strain and provocation. The decisive difficulty was Mrs. Gordon. Lindsay's mother was apparently neurotic, given to melancholia, religious obsessions, depression, and self-pity. We may feel certain that in all the family difficulties, and above all in those involving the son's low tastes and idle habits, the mother's attitude was a cardinal factor.

In hope of finding a therapeutic environment for his wife, Captain Gordon settled for a few years in the Azores. It was there that Adam Lindsay Gordon was born on October 19, 1833. But the Azores proved to be only a temporary location. Still in the hope of finding some settling influence for his wife, Captain Gordon took his family first to Madeira, and finally back to England and to Cheltenham. Young Lindsay was then nearly seven years old.

Gordon's schooling was spread over three schools and ten years. In 1841 he was entered as a day-boy at the newly founded Cheltenham College. He left the college in June of the next year, but seems to have returned later. At all events, in 1848 he was admitted to the Royal Military Academy at Woolwich, but he left in 1851 without completing his course. He then attended the Royal Worcester Grammar School for a time, in 1852.

Someone (it might have been Macaulay) is said to have declared to a youthful competitor who had beaten him at billiards:

"Young man, a reasonable proficiency at billiards is a graceful and gentlemanly accomplishment; but such proficiency as you have shown is the mark of a misspent life." Of Gordon's later prowess at Australian race-meetings this was literally true; the proficiency derived from a misspent youth. He did badly at his studies and gave his attention to boxing and horsemanship. In both activities he had professional supervision; Jem Edwards taught him to box and Tom Oliver taught him to ride. Edwards, a noted boxer, kept a sort of boxing studio in the Roebuck Inn at Cheltenham, where Gordon was an enthusiastic habitué. Tom Oliver was a famous steeplechase rider who had a racing-stable at Prestbury, near Cheltenham. He gave Gordon encouragement, coaching, and chances to ride. He was known as "Black Tom Oliver," because of his hair and complexion, and is mentioned by that name in Fytte II of "Ye Wearie Wayfarer." These two men may be said to have laid the foundations of Gordon's misfortunate career.

His family, and especially his mother, was displeased, not without reason. First, and most immediately important, was his neglect of his schooling; this could only bring about a failure which would leave him unqualified for any position either respectable or remunerative in the world of his time. There was a further objection. He was mixing in "low company." It is difficult for a later generation to enter fully into the feelings of the Gordons about their son's associations. Class distinctions were more rigid than they are now, and Cheltenham even in those days was a town especially sensitive to society and status. For these reasons, the idea began to take shape of sending Lindsay out of the country.

The notion of sending younger sons, ambitious youths, and ne'er-do-wells to find fortune or oblivion in the British possessions overseas was not a new one. For his own son, Captain Gordon had two alternatives in mind, India and Australia. The choice of Australia was probably due to the fact that he was able to provide letters of introduction to men of influence in South Australia. By the summer of 1853 the decision had been taken and the arrangements made.

At the same time, another complication developed in the inner life of the young man. He had fallen in love. He and Charley Walker, a boyhood friend, in their rides about the countryside, had made the acquaintance of a farmer named Bridges, who had two daughters, Jane and Sally. Sally was pretty and vivacious; Jane was beautiful (at least in Gordon's eyes), quiet and dignified. Gordon, like Walker, paid more attention to the talkative Sally, but he lost his heart to Jane.

On the eve of his departure he went to her and made a declaration. Even then, it was a declaration in limited, unimpassioned terms. He told her that if she would say the word he would refuse to go, would stay in England and try to make something of himself. She could not, or would not, say the word. She confessed that (in the conventional phrase) "there was another.". She left him on the doorstep, as she had been just leaving the house to go driving with her father, and Gordon went to Australia.

The character and conduct of Miss Bridges has been variously regarded. Miss Edith Humphris thought her a coolly calculating young woman who had made up her mind to marry money, and not to become involved with a man of no promise and few prospects, in disgrace with his own quite respectable family.[1] Yet no one can fairly blame her. Gordon's declaration, which can hardly be called a proposal, was indeed sudden. He had been distant, withdrawn, and uncommunicative toward her. Jane had had no reason to suspect in him any special feeling for herself. On every rational ground she was right in rejecting him. There was a barrier of class between them. Moreover, there is no evidence that she was fibbing when she said that her heart was no longer entirely her own.

The effect of the incident on Gordon is a matter of conjecture; there is reason to think that it was deep and lasting. In the poem "To My Sister," written just before his departure for Australia, three stanzas, the fifth, sixth, and seventh, obviously refer to Jane. They reflect disillusionment and disappointment ("I thought her breast as fair as snow, / 'Twas very near as cold"), mixed with romantic sadness ("And yet I may at times recall / Her memory with a sigh."). More significant evidence is the letter he wrote to Charley Walker a year and a half later, from Penola in South Australia: ". . . how is my old flame Jenny Bridges? I am as fond of her as ever and if she were out here I would certainly marry her *if she would have me*. She is just the sort of wife for the collonies [sic]. Love to her, regards to the governor."[2]

Gordon left England on August 7, 1853, in the 500-ton barque *Julia*. The voyage lasted fourteen weeks and was uneventful. About a month after sailing he wrote in a lady's album "An Exile's Farewell," a competent but undistinguished poem of seven eight-line stanzas, containing a repeated declaration that "I shed no tears at quitting home, / Nor will I shed them now!"

In an undated letter to Charley he mentions a shipboard flirtation with "a youngish married woman."[3] He may have been boasting. On November 14 he arrived in Adelaide.

II *Early Days in Australia*

Gordon's first action on arriving in Australia was characteristic, and negative. He refrained from presenting his letters of introduction, or making himself known to anyone who could have been of use to him. Instead, he applied for admission as a Mounted Trooper in the South Australian Mounted Police. This was on November 17, 1853, three days after his arrival. A week later, on November 24, he was accepted and became "P. T. Gordon," a gentleman-ranker.

He served in the Mounted Police for almost exactly two years. After an initial period of training at the Adelaide barracks, he was posted to the Mount Gambier region, a narrow pointed area between the border of Victoria and the eastern shore of the Great Australian Bight. His station was partly at Mount Gambier but mostly at Penola, a few miles to the north. It was here that his activities were centered through most of 1854 and 1855.

Af first he was happy in his new life. The undated letter to Charley Walker already referred to was evidently written soon after he had joined the Force. It is mainly cheerful in tone. He writes that he is getting on well and feeling fit. The new life suited him. He liked the out-of-doors and he liked horses; he now had plenty of both, undistracted by his family's ambitions for him or by any of the other problems of his earlier years. In any event, early days in a new land are normally full of interest and enjoyment, in the absence of homesickness or feelings of exile, and Gordon had firmly put such feelings behind him.

Gordon's career as a policeman was mostly made up of the usual routine of the country policeman. There are stories of his exploits and dangers which are mere legends. Some of them may be true; none are certainly so. What is important is that when he left the Force, in October, 1855, he stood well enough with his superiors so that there were official regrets and inquiries about his resignation.

On October 15, 1855, the Commissioner of Police addressed a memo to Inspector G. B. Scott concerning Gordon's resignation; he wished to know "*why* so steady and efficient a Trooper should be dissatisfied and wish to leave this honorable employment." Replying from Penola, on November 1, Inspector Scott wrote:

In answer to your "Memo" respecting the resignation of P. T. Gordon —I have the honour to inform you, that P. T. Gordon told me, he intended to turn his attention to driving cattle to market—I am not aware that he was dissatisfied with the "Police Force"—but I imagine he thinks it more lucrative to be a drover.

I am sorry to lose him, as he has conducted himself, [sic] remarkably well, while stationed here, which has been for a period of about eighteen months.[4]

There are three points worth noticing about this letter. First, it testifies to Gordon's efficiency as a policeman. Secondly, it implicitly denies that he had had, so far as the inspector knew, any unpleasantness to make him leave the Force. Thirdly, there seems to be just a little more in this than meets the eye, although it is not clear exactly what. Why did Gordon tell Scott that he was going "to be a drover"? He did not become a drover and it is not likely that he ever intended to become one. There are two main possibilities. One is that there really had been some unpleasantness which Gordon did not choose to reveal to his superior, preferring to let it be supposed that he had more lucrative employment in view. The other is that Gordon had merely grown tired of the routine life of a Mounted Trooper and decided to change to some more varied and individualistic way of life; in explanation, he gave his superior an off-hand reason which, though not scrupulously accurate, was true in its essentials.

For the next seven years he lived a nomadic, irregular and obscure life as a professional horse-breaker. During this period he made two new friendships and strengthened an old one.

He had come across William Trainor while in the Mounted Police, Trainor being then a performer in a circus. Trainor later left the circus and, like Gordon, turned to horse-breaking. At this time Gordon was living in a hut near Mount Gambier, where Trainor lived with him for some time. Together the two men talked, smoked, and read. Today, Trainor's body lies beside Gordon's in Brighton Cemetery.

At about the same time another young acquaintance appeared. Gordon began his career as a horse-breaker by working for Mr. Edward Stockdale, near Guichen Bay. Here he met young Harry Stockdale, who gave him good companionship and who later contributed reminiscences—sometimes inaccurate—of Gordon's life.

More important than either of these was the meeting in 1857 with the Reverend Julian Tenison Woods. Father Woods was a Roman Catholic missionary priest of broad interests, learning, and enthusiasm. Though his first intellectual interest was in natural history, he had a broad knowledge of literature, and, what was more, he had some books. He lent a volume of Horace to Gordon, who is said to have memorized most of the odes. This seems hard to believe, in view of the sketchy nature of Gordon's early education, but there seems no doubt about his remarkable rote-memory. Most importantly, his friendship with Father Woods was a renewed stimulus to the literary side of his nature and a reintroduction to serious literature and to the classics.

His life was lonely. It was at this time that he was most intensely *déclassé*. When he visited a station, he was not normally invited to share the manager's hospitality. Refusing to be relegated to the men's hut, he would make a camp by himself at some distance from the buildings. Here he would read for hours at night, by the dim light of a pannikin-lamp, holding the book very close on account of his nearsightedness.

Of what is vulgarly known as his "love-life" we do not know much. Australian life from its beginning involved a good deal of enforced celibacy. In Gordon's day the horse-breakers, stock-riders, and station-hands had little if any normal feminine society. Nubile aborigines were sometimes available and presumably some of the townships offered certain amenities. Occasionally, too, there would be lonely wives to be consoled.[5] None of this sort of thing would make a strong appeal to Gordon. He generally extended to women of all classes a chivalrous respect that must have been exasperating to a few of them. J. Howlett Ross quotes a significant reminiscence of Mrs. N. A. Lord's. As a girl, she would come out early in the mornings to watch Gordon training "Ingleside." One morning Gordon asked her if her mother knew about these visits, and on getting a negative answer asked her not to come again. He knew the world, he said, and she did not. It would not do.[6]

There is one matter which provokes curiosity. In his "Abbey Memorial Volume," Douglas Sladen refers to a mention by Turner and Sutherland of a "desperate flirtation which Gordon had in 1860 somewhere in the Mount Gambier district." He adds that he has had information about an illegitimate daughter of Gordon, who was still alive in 1912, somewhere near Mount Gambier.[7] At about the same time, Eileen Kaye published serially in the *Australasian* a "Life of Adam Lindsay Gordon." In the installment for October 7, 1933, she refers to two flirtations or courtships, with a "Mary McGougan" and a "Marie" at Bald Hills, adding that neither of these came to anything. But she

states that at the time of the purchase of the livery-stable at
Ballarat Gordon put £1000 in trust for "Marie." No authority is
given for this account, but if it is true its implications seem clear.

Not women, but horse-racing was Gordon's chief concern. He
is said to have traveled all over southeastern Australia—which
probably means eastern South Australia and western Victoria—
to compete in races. He earned money and he won local renown
as a rider, the nearest thing to fame that he was to receive during
his lifetime. This too turned to bitterness toward the end of his
life; it would be but a mild over-simplification to say that from
first to last horses were his ruin.

He rode only in steeplechases, never in flat races. His delight
was in jumping, whether in competition or not. As a Mounted
Policeman, he was noted for traveling by the most direct route
to wherever he had to go, jumping his horse over whatever bar-
riers happened to be along the way. Yet he was not by later
standards a good rider. He was loose and lanky in the saddle
("Long Gordon" was a recognized nickname) and in taking
jumps he would stretch his feet forward in the stirrups and lean
his body far back. He was also extraordinarily nearsighted. He
confessed that everything beyond his horse's ears was mere mist
and blur. He rode partly by intuition and partly by trusting his
horse and partly by not caring, to all appearances, whether he
broke his neck or not. It might be said that he did worse. He
suffered many hurts, mostly about the head, and the cumulative
effect of the battering his skull received was a predisposing
factor in his early death.

III *The Peak of Good Fortune*

Death seemed far enough away on October 20, 1862. On that
day he was married to Margaret Park, by the Reverend J. Dove,
at the manse at Mount Gambier, in the presence of Bradshaw
Young, Sergeant of Police, and Marie Young.

Maggie Park was born in Glasgow, the daughter of Alexander
Park, a baker by trade. She was brought as an infant to South
Australia, where her father found work as a shepherd and stone-
mason. Concerning the courtship and marriage there are the
usual legends and inaccuracies. An old story tells of how Gordon
had been injured in a fall, of how Maggie Park nursed him in
his convalescence and so won his heart and hand. The story was
contradicted sixty years later on the authority of the bride's sec-

ond husband. Peter Low's account, as reported in the Adelaide *Register* for October 5, 1922, suggests love at first sight.

The real question is: was it a good marriage or was it a mistake? It must be remembered that there were two sides to Gordon's life. One was that of the horseman and boxer, the man of action. Miss Park was a good horse-woman and therefore appealed to that side of Gordon. She was, in the Australian sense, a "mate" for him and he admired her for that.[8] The other side of Gordon was the literary, and on this side there was no contact at all between them. But it is not self-evident that a scholar needs a scholarly wife or a poet a poetical wife. Gordon's marriage seems to have been as wise a choice as he could have made. If there was a failure, it lay in this: Maggie did not have the combination of practical sense and force of character strong enough to steer her husband away from ruinous mistakes in the conduct of his affairs.

It was just at this time that Gordon's life took on a new and pleasurable aspect. He came into money. His mother had died early in 1859, leaving an estate of about £20,000. It took time, and some perseverance on the part of one of his uncles, to find the son who had gone to the antipodes. Lindsay Gordon's share was about £7,000, the equivalent of $33,500 in American money of today, and of two or three times that much, at least, in purchasing power.

Gordon now had both a fortune and a wife. In 1864-65, within twelve months, three further important events took place. In March of 1864 he bought the cottage near Fort Macdonell, known then and since as "Dingley Dell." This was the first and only real home that Gordon had, and he lived there but a short time. Later in the same year, 1864, Gordon's verse appeared, for the first time, in print. "Publication" seems too strong a term, but at the end of August *The Feud* was printed at Mount Gambier, even though in a small limited edition which hardly got beyond the doors of the print shop. Then, at the beginning of 1865, a deputation came to him to ask that he be a candidate for the Parliament of South Australia. He consented, was nominated, and by a very narrow margin won the election.

Gordon's parliamentary career was brief and undistinguished. He won friends, but influenced no one. He spoke in the House a dozen times, making no great impression either on his fellow-members or on the reporters who heard him. The speeches are more interesting to us today than they were to his contemporaries, who often found it hard to decide on which side Gordon

was trying to argue. The frequent Latin quotations neither en-
lightened nor impressed his hearers. He came to spend most of
his time making caricatures of the legislators of the day; these
gave him indeed a reputation, but not that of a serious politician.
What he valued most was the privilege of using the parliamentary
library. He would come there early in the day from his temporary home in the suburb of Glenelg, and would read until it was
time for the House to assemble. The business of parliament
bored him. In November, 1866, he resigned his seat.

There were at least two reasons for his resignation. He found
it dull to be a legislator. Debates, facts, statistics—the minutiae
of government held no appeal for him. But there was a practical
problem as well. He had made land-investments in Western
Australia which needed his personal attention. He would have to
be away from Adelaide for an indeterminate period. The only
fair course of action was for him to withdraw from the parliament and allow someone else to be chosen in his place.

The years 1862-66 were the apogee of Gordon's life. He was,
for the time being, well-off and respectable. Though his living-
quarters were modest, whether at Dingley Dell or in Penzance
Street, Glenelg, he had at least the semblance of a settled home,
a place to call his own. As a married man, a legislator and a
man of letters (at least in embryo) he held a recognized position in the community. Then came the fall, not swift but seem-
ingly irreversible, sudden and dramatic at its close.

IV   *Declining Fortunes*

At the end of 1866 Gordon went to Western Australia, ac-
companied by Lambton Mount. They took with them nearly five
thousand sheep. They landed at Bunbury and settled temporarily near Balingup, where they built miles of fencing to form
paddocks. Any sheep left outside the fence at night was lost to
the dingoes. Next, they moved to a more extensive location on
the Donnelly River, where they found a more dangerous enemy
than the dingoes. The poisonous blind grass, or Lobelia, was
thick on the ground, and became thicker and more dangerous
after Gordon's party had burnt off the undergrowth. The upshot
was that their flock was reduced to less than a third of its original
strength. Gordon gave up the project and came back east.[9]

Three months after his return, two volumes of his poetry were
published. On June 10, 1867, *Ashtaroth*, "by the author of *Sea
Spray and Smoke Drift*," appeared, to be followed nine days later

by *Sea Spray and Smoke Drift,* "by the author of *Ashtaroth.*" The
books did not sell. Financially, the venture was not a success and
was one more drain on Gordon's lessening resources.

What had become of the £7,000 he had inherited just before
his marriage? A good deal had been lost in the failure of his
sheep-farming venture in Western Australia. More had gone to
the purchase and upkeep of horses. Almost certainly, an indeterminate amount was given away, or lent with minimal hope
of repayment, to those whom he considered his friends. He was
as generous as he was unbusinesslike. The publication of his
two volumes of poetry took a little more, and brought no return.
So, although he was still far from penniless, he had cause for uneasiness in the rate at which his capital was diminishing.

The question of money and occupation was therefore becoming serious. In plain terms, he needed a job, and getting one was
anything but easy. He had but two skills to offer: one was literature and the other was the handling of horses. He was growing dissatisfied with the second, and Australia offered little scope
for the first. In 1867 he is said to have planned the writing of a
novel, but the scheme came to nothing.[10] A couple of years later
(after the period now under review) he was offered a journalistic post as a sports reporter for the *Australasian.* He refused it
because the work would have led him into further and closer
association with the sporting crowd from which he was increasingly anxious to break loose.[11]

At this time a possible source of livelihood, perhaps even of
affluence, came to his attention. Craig's Hotel, in Ballarat, had a
livery stable attached to it, and the business was at this time to
let. It looked like a good opening for Gordon. He understood
horses and he was well known among men who rode and drove
horses. The business had flourished in the past. It must have
been with good hopes for the future that Gordon assumed owner-
ship of the business and a leasehold of the stables, in November,
1867. He established himself and his family in a cottage by Lake
Wendouree, in Ballarat.

Once again there was failure where there ought to have been
success. And once again, the cause lay in Gordon's inability to
deal with the routine requirements of day-to-day living. He was
too easily bored as well as too easily imposed upon. Though the
livery-stable seemed to prosper, Gordon did not, because he did
not collect the debts that were due him. Nor did he keep his
accounts with the care which a successful business demands. Then
he took a partner—and chose a man apparently as feckless as

himself. Harry Mount was a brother of Lambton Mount, who had gone with Gordon to Western Australia. He kept the firm's books as confusedly as Gordon himself had done. By the time spring came, he was in debt. The livery-stable could not be made to pay under his methods of management.

Then another stroke of good luck intervened. He received two small legacies, one from a cousin and one from his grandmother. These gave him enough money to pay his debts. He gave up the livery-stable and left Ballarat with honor but without much else.

This was at the beginning of October, 1868. For the next six months he was again homeless. His wife had gone to visit her family, her father being ill, and Gordon was alone. From Ballarat he went to spend a couple of months with Robert Power. In December he was with the officers of the Fourteenth Regiment in the St. Kilda Barracks, Melbourne. Early in the new year he went to Yallum, where he spent at least three months with the Riddochs. At the end of March, 1869, he arranged for lodgings at 10 Lewis Street, in Brighton, a suburb of Melbourne.

The Lewis Street house was Gordon's last place of residence. His landlady was Mrs. Kelly, whose husband was gardener to a Melbourne barrister named Higginbotham. It may have been Higginbotham who initiated the arrangement. At any rate, he took an interest in his gardener's lodger, and lent him books. Gordon, for his part, when he was not working with horses, wrote, walked, and swam off Brighton Beach.

V *Catastrophe*

The sequence of events which led directly to Gordon's death had already begun. About the beginning of October, 1868,[12] he got word from Scotland that he was, or might be, the lawful heir to the estate of Esslemont, in Aberdeenshire. The estate had been left by will to the daughter of a previous owner, Huntley Gordon. But the estate had been entailed, and under the entail the testamentary disposition was invalid. If it held, Gordon was the lawful, though dispossessed, owner of an estate supposed to be worth £2000 a year.

Everything depended on the entail. If it held, Gordon was entitled to the property. But entails had been broken or set aside, and an Act of 1848 had done away with certain kinds of entail altogether. There were thus questions of law to be answered: Did the Act of 1848 affect the estate of Esslemont? Had the specific entail on Esslemont been legally set aside at any time in the past?

At first, Gordon paid little attention to the matter, for two reasons. The first was an initially pessimistic view of his prospects. He felt that the prospect held out was too good to be true; there must be a catch in it somewhere, and he wrote as much to Riddoch in October, 1868. The second reason was a gentlemanly reluctance to dispossess the lady who had received the property by testamentary disposition some four years earlier.

Two causes led him to change his mind. Early in 1869 he received information that the lady in possession, Ann Wolrige, was wealthy in her own right and would suffer no grave injury by being deprived of Esslemont. Secondly, and inevitably, he began to feel how desirable it would be if his claim were made good and he were to come into a large and secure income. In this feeling there was neither avarice nor egoism. He believed that he had not many years to live. Moreover, he had no son, and no chance of beginning a new Gordon dynasty. But he did have one hope, which led him on. He saw that if he could establish his claim to Esslemont and then live for just a few years longer, he could put by enough money so that his widow would be well provided for after his death. This was his central, conscious purpose.

The first step was to find the answer to the second of the two questions already stated. Had the entail on Esslemont ever been broken? He was advised to consult Mr. J. C. Stewart, a Melbourne lawyer with special competence in Scottish law. Mr. Stewart worked up a case to be presented for counsel's opinion in Edinburgh, to a specialist in the law of entail. The first report was favorable. The entail on Esslemont had never been broken. So far, Gordon's claim was firmly based. The next step was to establish it, in the courts if necessary, and get possession of the property.

During this last period of his life, Gordon was living in Brighton, the suburb to the south of Melbourne. He had two projects to occupy his mind: the securing of a valuable property, and the preparation of a new volume of poems. His body was mainly active in walking and swimming, and in a limited exercise of horsemanship. His moods we know little about. It is unlikely that they were consistently cheerful. He had forebodings, probably of the near future—certainly of the more distant future. His body, especially his head, had been battered by repeated injuries. All his enterprises had so far come to failure, largely through the negligence or unwisdom of his own rebellious spirit. And he was going deeper in debt than ever. This was

partly due to the prosecution of his claim to Esslemont. Litiga-
tion, at every step and in any form, costs money. Also, his ex-
pectation of future affluence made him a little more willing to
incur debts for the expenses of daily living and to let his bills
run on—and up. After all, he had no clear alternative. He simply
had no way of making a living save one, and he had taken a
deep dislike to that one. He wanted to get away from horses, not
because he had turned against horses but because of the company they drew him into.

This was the situation in mid-June, 1870. Then the blow fell.
About June 20 (Moir places it on the 23rd) a letter came from
Scotland. Esslemont was not to be his. An earlier case had been
decided in such a way as to make it clear that the class of entail
to which Esslemont belonged had been abolished by the Act of
1848. To make the unwelcome assurance doubly sure, this earlier
case had been appealed to the Privy Council, which had sus-
tained the decision.

Thus, in a few minutes, Gordon's world was turned upside-
down. The change from high hopes to hopelessness was as dras-
tic as a doctor's death sentence. His debts were serious, for
Gordon not only had no money but could see no way of getting
any. Even if he had been willing to go on training horses, only
a combination of luck with drudgery would have enabled him
to recoup his losses, pay his debts, and support himself and his
wife. His only other interest in life was literature, which did not
pay. He had refused a journalistic post for the same reason as
made him wish to give up steeplechasing. He was wearily eager
to escape from that kind of life and that kind of people.

Literature was indeed, just at this time, an added financial
burden to him. He had put together a new book of poems, *Bush
Ballads and Galloping Rhymes,* which was published on June 23,
1870, by Clarson, Massina & Co., of Melbourne. The expenses of
publication were Gordon's responsibility, and on that day he
called at the publishers' office and got the bill. It was no great
surprise to him; he must have known, from past experience,
about what it would be. Only, the concreteness of the written
statement underscored the unpalatable hopeless facts.

He was temporarily cheered by meetings with Marcus Clarke
and with Henry Kendall. He especially liked and admired Kendall. The two men had a lengthy talk in a convenient tavern.
Kendall had been given proof-sheets of *Bush Ballads and Galloping Rhymes,* and had written an enthusiastic review of the book
for publication in the *Australasian.* He showed Gordon the re-

view, also in proof. This gave a temporary lift to his spirits, but pointed to no solution of his problems. It was pleasant to know that a fellow-poet whom he respected thought his verses good; it was no guarantee that they would sell. Kendall was as poor as he, despite six years' steady employment in the Civil Service. And Gordon still owed more than £400.

In the evening, Gordon went home to his lodgings in Brighton. What time he reached Lewis Street, or how he spent the rest of the evening, or whether he slept well or badly, we do not know. We can only guess the state of his mind. We can legitimately imagine him sitting all night in the chair in front of a dying fire, brooding on an unthinkable future while his wife slept in her bed. Afterward, she remembered being half-awakened by a parting kiss, in the morning.

By morning, if no sooner, his mind was made up. Earlier in the year he had joined the Brighton Artillery Corps, and he had in his possession a rifle and some ammunition belonging to the Corps. So armed, he went out into the winter dawn, heading toward Picnic Point, on the southerly stretch of Brighton Beach. He walked down Park Street from the Marine Hotel to the beach. He sat down among the scrub and, in all likelihood, smoked a last pipe. He placed the pipe, and a shilling, in the crater of his hat, which he laid on the ground beside him. He got a forked twig from a ti-tree, long enough for his purpose. Lastly, he put the muzzle of the loaded rifle in his mouth and with the forked twig sprung the trigger. The bullet went through his brain, and his life and his problems were ended. It was June 24, 1870. Midwinter on Brighton Beach.

Later in the morning the body was found by a chance passer-by and taken at first to the Marine Hotel. The burial was in Brighton Cemetery. Then, in October, some of his friends and admirers had a gravestone erected. It took the form of a fluted column, broken off to symbolize his early death, and encircled just below the break by a laurel wreath. The column rises from a square plinth, on three sides of which were inscribed the titles of his three books. On the fourth side, in front, facing the path, was placed the inscription: "THE / POET / GORDON / DIED JUNE 24, 1870 / AGED 37 YEARS." A wattle tree was planted by the grave, in accord with the closing lines of "The Sick Stockrider": "Let me slumber in the hollow where the wattle blossoms wave. . . ." For years the symbolic wattle was maintained, and replaced when necessary, by Mrs. Elizabeth Lauder, one of his fondest admirers. It is there no longer; the grave-site is a clean-swept area of sand, stone, and gravel.

It might be said of Gordon that "Nothing in his life / Became him like the leaving it." He achieved by the manner of his dying the fame which he had missed in his lifetime. Not only fame, but posthumous success came to him. People began to buy his books, which were reprinted, reissued, re-edited, collected, recollected, selected, and anthologized, for more than forty years, and sporadically thereafter. Although the best-known collected edition was published before World War I, it still remains in print. Besides, a great deal of energy has gone into the perpetuation of his memory. There have been pilgrimages to the Gordon Cottage at Ballarat, now located in the public gardens of that city and serving also as a Gordon museum. Dingley Dell has been preserved as the principal Gordon museum, not many miles from the obelisk at Blue Lake which bears his name. A statue of Gordon near the Parliament House in Melbourne was unveiled in the presence of a large and distinguished audience on October 30, 1932. Most remarkable of all is the bust in the Poet's Corner, Westminster Abbey, unveiled by the Duke of York (later King George VI) on May 11, 1934, on which occasion the address was delivered by the Most Reverend Cosmo Gordon Lang, the Archbishop of Canterbury. Gordon is the only writer from the "British Dominions beyond the seas" to be so honored.

All these honors, all this publicity produced the inevitable reaction. The Abbey bust gives him the title, "National Poet of Australia," but there were those who said that he was not much of a poet, and there were those who said that he was even less of an Australian. One fact, however, is clear: no Australian poet to this day has made such a strong impact on the Australian consciousness, or to such a wide audience. Although bilious nationalists may call him an immigrant and fastidious critics may call him a scribbler, the truth is that for three generations he was, *de facto*, the national poet, the Australian Tennyson, the best-known and most-quoted writer of nineteenth-century Australia.

VI *Postscript on His Character*

The foregoing sketch of Gordon's life may give some indication of the kind of man he was. There were, however, some aspects of his character which call for more explicit comment.

One quality that stands out in his make-up is a lonely reticence. He consistently avoided putting his name to his published writings. *The Feud* was printed under the transparent pseudonym of "A. Lindsay." The three following books were all published as "By the Author of . . ." For his newspaper pieces he used various pen names. His whole life was a withdrawn and lonely one, its loneliness modified by a few friendships which were warm without being intimate. Charley Walker, William Trainor, Tenison Woods, Harry Stockdale, Bradshaw Young—not one of these was at all close to his mind or feelings, with the partial exception of Father Woods. His wife was little, if any, closer. She had no part in the literary side of his life. She observed him "scribbling poetry most of the time," or "writing poetry every evening, and in spare moments during the day," and that was all. "At the best of times he was uncommunicative . . . ." she said; and again, "He never spoke much of his family. Indeed, he did not speak much about anything. He was very reticent, and he did not like anyone prying into his affairs."[13]

Without much doubt, this solitary bent of his mind contributed to the making of his poetry. Poetry was his outlet, his way of working off the moods and ideas which he could not talk about. The late T. S. Eliot has testified that a poet may write to get rid of some emotion, or experience, or obsession which continues to be a discomfort until it is exorcised by being formulated in the words of a poem.[14] Poetry may have been Gordon's way of cleansing his "stuffed bosom of that perilous stuff / Which weighs upon the heart." Certainly, he had no other.

His attitude to women has already been noted.[15] Chastity and sobriety were among his fundamental qualities. There may have been lapses; presumably there were, although the evidence is far from conclusive. There still exists a legend that he drank heavily, at least toward the close of his life. But the record is against it. George Gordon McCrae, for example, wrote of "Gordon's avoidance of liquor; which, in the midst of all-round drinking society, had the effect of keeping him very much outside."[16]

He was always, in some sense, "outside," because of one fundamental contradiction in himself, the conflict between the gentleman and the "fellow," who seemed both to inhabit the same skin. Gordon was a gentleman by birth, by the expectations of his family, and by such schooling as he had. He never really forgot that he was a gentleman, either. That was why, as a horse-breaker, he chose to camp by himself rather than risk the snub of being sent to the "men's" quarters. He put himself down as a "Gent." on his marriage certificate. In the racing-programs of the time, where other riders were listed as "Smith" or "Jones," Gordon appears as "Mr. Gordon."

On the other hand, he had a habit from his school days of seeking associates among the "lower orders." Boxers and jockeys were his heroes. When he arrived in Australia, he avoided all contact with the men of substance to whom he had letters of introduction, and spent the first decade of his life there with policemen, horsemen, and stockriders. The chief exception was itself significant. Father Tenison Woods was a scholar and a priest, but he was a Roman Catholic and therefore not quite the gentleman, socially, that a C. of E. clergyman would have been. Later, at Ballarat, Gordon associated by choice with stable-boys, and talked about horses. He was never willing to talk about literature except with Father Woods, and, toward the end of his life, with Henry Kendall and Marcus Clarke.

The result of this ambivalence in Gordon was suggested by William Brazenor, in an interview published in the Melbourne *Argus* for October 11, 1913. "He was a man I could never make out. He was in no way a sociable man; far from it. . . . Gordon always gave me the idea that he had got out of his place in the world, and was mixing with people who were not of his class. He had the look of a man who had lost himself." We are familiar with the "quest for identity" as a literary theme; in Gordon we are confronted with a real-life specimen of a man who lacks a clear sense of his own identity. There was an unresolved dichotomy at the center of his being. He could not belong in the world of the gentry, but he could not abandon it either. He was neither a gentleman nor a not-gentleman. In the past, he had chosen the life of a hired vagabond and rejected the possibilities of secure respectability in a black coat; yet he could not wholly detach himself from the world of gentility or from the assumptions among which he had lived his earliest years. It is a good thing to have, like Kim, two sides to one's head, but not when they begin to quarrel with each other.

His religion was a vacuum. He did not have the poetic pantheism of Swinburne or Meredith, and still less did he possess the frank, joyous, aggressive paganism associated with the names of Hugh McCrae and Norman Lindsay. The Reverend P. J. Malone, years after Gordon's death, wrote of his great lack of faith, or reverence, or awe, and described his philosophy as a "cheerless agnosticism" and a "savage heroism."[17] F. W. L. Adams, writing much earlier, had seen Gordon as a product of his age, one who had lost the old faith and could not find a new one, and a victim of "the doubt and bewilderment of a period of transition."[18] The conventional religious training of his early youth had failed him. His mother's instability may well have given him a bias against religion. Nothing that touched his life in Australia, whether sacred or secular, was designed to open for him any visions of a hyper-phenomenal reality or to enable him to see the world *sub specie aeternitatis*.

Two minor points may be stated, or restated. First, his remarkable rote-memory gave him a knowledge of literature out of all proportion to his opportunities. Secondly, he had a physical and mental indolence which affected him whenever he was not in the excitement of horse-training, or racing, or poetic composition. He simply could not work at anything which did not spontaneously call out his interest. And over all was a perpetual and brooding melancholy.

VII *Summary of Gordon's Publications*

Gordon published three volumes of poetry in his lifetime. This is without counting *The Feud*, which, though it was printed at Mount Gambier in 1864, can hardly be said to have been "published" then, since most of the copies were packed away unbound.[19]

His first real book came out on June 10, 1867. It was a long, awkward, rather dull and pretentious poem called *Ashtaroth, a Dramatic Lyric*, "by the Author of *Sea Spray and Smoke Drift*," published by Clarson, Massina & Co., of Melbourne. One lyric section, now known as "Thora's Song," had been previously published in the *Australasian* for January 19, 1867, under the title "Frustra," and was later excerpted to form the final item in Gordon's last book of poems. The work as a whole was ignored at the time and has not been highly regarded since.

Only nine days separated Gordon's first book from his second, *Sea Spray and Smoke Drift*, which was published on June 19, 1867. The title-page stated that it was "by the author of Ashtaroth," and that the publisher was George Robertson.[20] Thus, within a fortnight, Gordon published two books of verse, under the imprints of two different publishers, and each declared to be "by the author of" the other.

Sea Spray and Smoke Drift was quite a different sort of book from its predecessor. It was a collection of twenty-three poems, of which two, "Ye Wearie Wayfarer" and "Hippodromania," were divided into separately titled sections. The eight "Fyttes" of "Ye Wearie Wayfarer" and five parts of "Hippodromania" had appeared earlier, in the *Australasian* and in *Bell's Life in*

Victoria, respectively; a shorter poem,, "Ars Longa," had been
printed in the *Border Watch* a few weeks previously to the
book's publication. This second volume had one thing in common with the first; it was, for all practical purposes, unnoticed
and unbought.

During the three years that separated the second from the
third of Gordon's books, he wrote a few prose pieces for publication in the *Australasian,* notably one called "Racing Ethics"
(April, 1868) and anther called "The Ring and the Books" (July,
1869). These appeared under the pseudonym of "Turfcutter."
More important, a few alert readers were becoming aware of
him as a writer of verse. Then, on June 12, 1869, "How We Beat
the Favourite" was published in the *Australasian,* to be followed
six months later by "The Sick Stockrider." These two poems took
the public fancy, and prepared the way for the rush of popularity
that came after his death.

In 1870 Gordon put together his third book, *Bush Ballads and
Galloping Rhymes,* containing sixteen poems, of which one, "The
Road to Avernus," was divided into six sections with separate
subtitles. The most ambitions pieces—and the longest except for
"The Road to Avernus"—were "The Rhyme of Joyous Garde" and
"The Romance of Britomarte." Two of the poems, as we have
just seen, were already known from the pages of the *Australasian.* Two others, "Wolf and Hound" and "A Song of Autumn,"
had recently been printed in the same periodical, and "Doubtful
Dreams" had appeared in the *Colonial Monthly* as early as December 1, 1868. This third and final book was published on June
23, 1870.

As well as the poems in Gordon's three books—or four, if we
were to count *The Feud*—there are others which came to light
after his death. Some of these were early verses, such as "To My
Sister" and "An Exile's Farewell," written respectively before and
during his voyage to Australia. Others were random verses written in Australia, such as "Argemone," written for Miss Riddoch
at the end of 1869. They are to be found in the various collected
editions which appeared in the decades following the poet's
death.

Two of the poems posthumously attributed to Gordon are now
generally rejected from the canon. The first was called "A Fragment," sixteen lines long, beginning "They say that poison-
sprinkled flowers . . .", which appears, for example, on page 228
of *Poems by Adam Lindsay Gordon,* published in 1898 at London by Robt. A. Thompson & Co., Ltd., and at Melbourne by

A. H. Massina & Co. These lines were included at one time in the Robb edition, first issued in 1912, but were dropped from later printings. In fact, they are substantially the same as—though not identical with—those in Aytoun's *Bothwell*, Part II, Section XVIII, lines 513-24, 529-32 (Aytoun's *Poems;* Oxford, 1921, p. 162).

The second case is more confused. A poem of fifteen eight-line stanzas in the style of Gordon and first called "Under the Trees" was published early in 1871, first in the *South Australian Register* and again, a month later, in the *Australasian*. It appeared again in May, 1873, in *Temple Bar,* where it was given the title "A Voice from the Bush," by which title it has been generally known since. It was included in the collected editions of Gordon's poems from 1880 to 1894. The real author was almost certainly a Mr. Mowbray Morris, who claimed to have written the verses "in a cave at Robe in the autumn of 1871"; E. M. Robb quotes his letter in the current Oxford edition of Gordon's poems (page 364). Miss Edith Humphris, in her *Life of Adam Lindsay Gordon* (pages 45 f., 142) argues for Gordon's authorship, but she depends on reminiscences set down years after the event by people only indirectly concerned. Arguments from the text are inconclusive.

To sum up, we have from Gordon three books of poetry, plus *The Feud,* plus about a dozen miscellaneous pieces which have been added over the years to the collected editions. These are the works to be considered.

CHAPTER 2

The Pattern of the Poetry

I *On Poetry in General*

THERE is no clear answer to the question, What is poetry? From Aristotle to T. S. Eliot there has been much comment and explication, but no agreed definition. Wordsworth, for example, provides us with phrases about "emotion recollected in tranquillity" and "the spontaneous overflow of powerful feelings," but phrases such as these do not help to define poetry; at best, they help to describe it. Shelley, in the *Defense of Poetry*, speaks of poetry in terms equally applicable to prose fiction or even to ballet dancing. The critics of the twentieth century, for all their efforts, succeed no better.

We have, therefore, some right to set up a simplified *rationale* of poetry, such as may give us a useful basis for discussion. The first fact about poetry is that it is the use of language in the particular fashion that we call "verse." That is to say, it is in language which has been organized into a predictable rhythmic pattern, with or without the added sound recurrences of rhyme. These are the means, but to what end are they used? The real nature of anything is to be found in its purposes.

It is universally admitted that poetry is to give "pleasure," or "delight." Wordsworth and Eliot are at one on this point.[1] Poetry must then meet some need, satisfy some desire of our psychic natures, as food satisfies the need of our physical natures. Three of these needs can be identified. The first is the need for storytelling. Children and adults alike want stories. The popularity of novels in the modern world testifies to this, as does the predominance of the epic and the ballad in the earlier stages of civilization. The second need is that for expressing ideas, or reflections. Our minds want to comment, and to generalize, and some of this activity is shaped into verse and becomes poetry. The popular proverb at one end of the scale and the philoso-

30

phical-religious purposes of *The Four Quartets* enclose between them an almost endless variety of reflective content in poetry. This reflective content is not necessarily, nor even usually, directly expressed. At its best, it comes to us through some form of narrative. In this way, we are given an ethical system in *The Faerie Queene*, a theological system in *Paradise Lost*, and an aesthetic theory in *Fra Lippo Lippi*. The third need is for the expression of emotion, and for sympathy with the common passions of human life. For many readers this is the prime function of poetry, if not its only function. Its importance is not to be denied. We are emotional creatures, and we are, in a literal sense, desperately inarticulate. When the poets are able to lend us words for the expression of our feelings they deserve our thanks; and if they enable us to enter sympathetically into the emotions of others and to share more vividly the common stock of human experience, so much the better.

We accept then, for our purpose, three functions of poetry and three kinds of poetry to correspond: namely, the narrative, the reflective, and the emotive. These three are separable but not necessarily separate. The most rewarding poetry fulfills all three purposes at once. Narrative poetry is charged with emotion. If it were not, it would not interest us. Conversely, emotions are best conveyed to us through narrative. It was not a lyricist but a dramatist of whom Matthew Arnold wrote that "all griefs which bow / Find their sole speech in that victorious brow." Moreover, the poetic statement of ideas is most effectively made through narrative. This has been the way of the poets.

There is one other sort of poetry that needs to be kept in mind when dealing with poetry of the late nineteenth century in either Australia or North America. Descriptive poetry, or landscape poetry, is markedly conspicuous. This descriptive poetry is related to the other categories in two ways. First, it is, or may be, a part of narrative. It may also be emotive, and generally is. It expresses a feeling for the landscape, or it is used as a springboard for the expression of other feelings, such as loneliness, or nostalgia.

There is, then, narrative poetry; there is reflective poetry; and there is emotional poetry. With this framework in mind we turn to a general examination of the body of Gordon's poetry.

II *On Gordon's Poetry*

In Gordon's two volumes, excluding both *The Feud* and *Ashtaroth*, and counting separately the named sections of poems so divided, there are fifty-five poems. Of these, sixteen are straight-forward narratives, including such well-known poems as "The Rhyme of Joyous Garde," "How We Beat the Favourite," and "Wolf and Hound." Twelve others might be called semi-narra-tive; these are not primarily storytelling poems, but have a narra-tive basis or a strong narrative element. "The Sick Stockrider" might be called a narrative poem, but its narrative content is not organized into a story; it is used for a different purpose. "Podas Okus" is a meditation, part soliloquy and part monologue, but it has a narrative foundation. Two of the "Fragmentary Scenes" from "The Road to Avernus" are narrative fragments. In all, fewer than one-third of the poems are unambiguously narrative; almost exactly one-half are of the narrative sort.

If we were to estimate bulk rather than numbers, the propor-tions would be altered. If we were to add *Ashtaroth* and *The Feud*, and count pages instead of titles, we would find that about three-quarters of the verse would be classed as narrative.

Gordon is remembered about equally for his narrative and for his reflective verse. On one hand, the present writer remembers well his first meeting with one of the leading living authorities on Australian literature, who, when the name of Adam Lindsay Gordon came into the conversation, quoted immediately and with gusto the closing lines of "How We Beat the Favourite." On the other hand, as for the world over, the best-known lines of all are the quatrain beginning "Life is mostly froth and bubble" from Fytte VIII of "Ye Wearie Wayfarer." Thousands of people have known those lines who have never heard of Adam Lindsay Gordon.[2] This Fytte, we might add, is subtitled "A Metaphysical Song."

To set a proportion of reflective poems among the total is more difficult than for the narratives. For one thing, the classes over-lap. "The Sick Stockrider" is in one sense narrative, but it is remembered principally for the meditations on life which are implicit in the second-last stanza. We can classify eleven of the poems as reflective, or "philosophical" (the quotation marks are necessary) in their main intent. These are exemplified by "Finis Exoptatus," the final Fytte of "Ye Wearie Wayfarer." Five more might be considered as partly reflective, making a total of sixteen.

Poems of emotion are still more difficult to classify, since all poems are emotional except the comic. What is here meant by an "emotional" poem is one of which the primary purpose is the direct expression of feelings, such expression as Keats gives in the sonnet "On First Looking into Chapman's Homer." Ten of the poems in Gordon's two volumes (exclusive, that is, of *Ashtaroth*) are, in this sense, poems of emotion, exemplified by "Whisperings in Wattle Boughs" or "A Song of Autumn." The proportion is higher among the miscellanenous poems that were added in later collected editions, poems such as "An Exile's Farewell" and "To a Proud Beauty."

Something remains to be said about descriptive poetry. In the poetry of the English-speaking colonies during the nineteenth century there was a curious preponderance of nature description. This was more marked in Canada than elsewhere, but the tendecy existed also in Australia and in South Africa. This kind of poetry, indeed, seems more prominent than it really was, because it was the kind that most noticeably survived in anthologies. Examples include Charles Harpur's "A Midsummer Noon in the Australian Forest," Henry Kendall's "Bell-Birds," and J. L. Cuthbertson's "The Bush." These are all to be found in *A Book of Australian and New Zealand Verse*, chosen by Sir Walter Murdoch and Alan Mulgan, and published by the Oxford University Press in four editions from 1918 to 1920. In South African collections it is a little less conspicuous, but it is there. The best-known example is Thomas Pringle's "Afar in the Desert," which is included as a matter of course in the South African anthology published by the Oxford Press in 1959, with introduction by Guy Butler.[3] In Canadian poetry the incidence of nature-description is higher. Poems such as W. W. Campbell's "Indian Summer," or Archibald Lampman's "Heat," are among the most frequently chosen selections to represent the typical Canadian poetry of the nineteenth century.

Gordon's poems have relatively little of this, as we shall see later on. There is not one which is compounded throughout of nature-description without any human interest at all. There are Canadian poets who do this, as Campbell has done in "Indian Summer," but Gordon does not. The nearest approach to it is the "Dedication" which opens the final volume, *Bush Ballads and Galloping Rhymes*. Besides this, of course, he often uses the familiar method of beginning a poem with some description, as Wordsworth does in "Michael" and Tennyson in "Oenone." In all, there are no more than fourteen poems which are descriptive to any degree worth considering. Allowing for the amount of description which poets, novelists, and essayists ordinarily use for various purposes, and taking into account the purely descriptive verse that was composed elsewhere during the period, this seems a modest proportion.

In these estimates we have considered almost entirely the two collections that were published in Gordon's lifetime, with the omission of *Ashtaroth*. The omission is dictated by the fact that *Ashtaroth* is in a class by itself. It is a long dramatic poem, and is therefore basically narrative. It is not, however, an engrossing narrative, and few have read it for the sake of the story. Few, indeed, have a good word to say for it, except that the five stanzas known as "Thora's Song," reprinted under that title in *Bush Ballads and Galloping Rhymes*, have a lyric attractiveness. The poem is different in kind from the other two books and cannot be summarized in the same way. It will call for special consideration later.

We shall now look at Gordon's poetry under the three headings already set down. There is his narrative poetry, and his reflective poetry, and his emotional poetry. The three elements do overlap and criss-cross to a considerable extent. This is not altogether disadvantageous. It means that we shall sometimes have occasion to look at the same poem from different standpoints. The stereoscopic view is always the more revealing.

CHAPTER 3

The Narratives

EXCLUSIVE of *The Feud* and *Ashtaroth,* and leaving out of account a few minor examples, there are a dozen poems which are clear narratives, six in each of the two main volumes. The most obvious fact about them is the division into two kinds, according to the material Gordon used. Some of the stories belong to an old, exotic world of Arthurian legend, of border balladry, of Cavalier swashbuckling, and even of Spanish bullfighting. The others are of Gordon's own time and mostly of Gordon's own world. "How We Beat the Favourite" and "The Roll of the Kettledrum" belong to England and the Crimea, respectively, so far as the locale is concerned. But the latter is an English story although most of the action takes place far from England, and the former is in tone and spirit an Australian story even though it happened in England. The rest belong altogether to Australia.

I Stories from the Past

We shall begin by examining the most ambitious of the narratives in the old style, "The Romance of Britomarte," from *Bush Ballads and Galloping Rhymes.* It is a story of Cavaliers and Roundheads, set evidently in the latter part of the year 1644, after the Battle of Marston Moor, and told in thirty stanzas of ten lines each. The structure of these stanzas is itself interesting and original. Gordon uses a four-beat line with a mixture of iambic and anapaestic feet which makes for a lively and flexible rhythm appropriate to the spirit of the poem. Each stanza consists of two quatrains with alternate rhyme, and a couplet at the end; that is, the rhyme-scheme is *a b a b c d c d e e.* He rhymes the name of "Gwendoline" to "between," "clean," "ween," and "been." All these rhymes except the last sounds odd to a modern reader, but while we admit that Gordon's ear was sometimes uncertain in the matter of rhyme we ought also to remember that the pronunciation of proper names varies considerably from place to place and from time to time.

A notable feature of the poem is the use which is made of a refrain-like repetition. The line, "For the glory of God and of Gwendoline," occurs three times in the poem, as the final lines of stanzas four, twelve, and sixteen; then, at the close of stanza twenty-six, we have "The wedding of Guy and of Gwendoline." This is counterpointed by five other stanza-closing lines ending each with the name of "Britomarte."

> Of the bravest of destriers, 'Britomarte.' (Stanza 1)
> For their gold and silver, with Britomarte. (Stanza 6)
> I could baffle them all upon Britomarte. (Stanza 11)
> At the folly of following Britomarte. (Stanza 17)
> The story of *her* and of Britomarte. (Stanza 30)

The effect of these two schemes of repetition is to give the "feel" of an Old Ballad without the obvious device of a formal refrain.

The story is told "as related by Sergeant Leigh on the night he got his captaincy at the Restoration," according to the subtitle. The narrator is thus looking back over an interval of sixteen years. He is himself the hero of the tale, which he tells in the first person.

> I'll tell you a story: but pass the "jack,"
>   And let us make merry to-night, my men.
> Aye, those were the days when my beard was black—
>   I like to remember them now and then.

Sir Hugh, the lord of St. Hubert's Chase, had been killed at Edgehill. A garrison placed at his estate was needed elsewhere and withdrawn. After the Royalist defeat at Marston Moor, Ralph Leigh rode to the house alone "through the moonlit park." Sir Hugh's wife and infant son were both dead, leaving as the heiress his daughter Gwendoline, a former playmate of Leigh's:

> I have carried her miles when the woods were wet,
>   I have read her romances of dame and knight;
>   She was my princess, my pride, my pet.

In addition there were in the house Old Miles, three troopers, and the chatelaine, Mistress Ruth, a "mettlesome soul," half-sister to Sir Hugh.

Leigh's purpose in coming to St. Hubert's Chase was to bring a warning against a marauding band of Roundheads. He had made his way successfully through hostile country, thanks to the speed of his "brave brown mare," Britomarte. He found that the defense of the mansion depended on fewer than ten men servants, five soldiers, and a useless cannon. Soon, John Kerr and his Roundheads arrived and demanded the surrender of the mansion "in the people's name." Dame Ruth was strong for resistance, but the place would not be able to hold out for long. The defenders were outnumbered and outgunned. The only hope lay in relief, and to get that someone would have to "break through the rebel force" and ride to Westbrooke, where Lord Guy had four troops of horse-soldiers. Ralph Leigh undertook the mission, "for the glory of God and of Gwendoline."

Lightly armed, with drawn sword, Leigh on Britomarte bounded out of the postern gate. The rebels shot at him, but missed. One sergeant got close enough to have his skull split by Leigh's sword. Britomarte carried Leigh through the park, over the boards and dyke that fenced it, and swiftly on to Westbrooke. Though weak from loss of blood (the poem does not make clear how he got his wound) he rode back with Lord Guy's troopers and took part in the fight that followed. In ten minutes all the Roundheads had been dispersed, captured, or killed. John Kerr was one of the captured; the victors hanged him as a traitor and a turncoat. Britomarte dies, presumably of exhaustion. Ralph Leigh got a kiss from Gwendoline, and a braid of her hair, as a reward. After the action he became unconscious, from the effects of his wound and of the excitement, and he remained so for three weeks. When he recovered he learned that Gwendoline had been married to Lord Guy.

The poem is rounded off with a sketch of the subsequent narrative. Of the four soldiers in the original group at St. Hubert's, three are dead; the fourth, Holdsworth, survived; "at least he was living two years ago." But Gwendoline the "maiden wonderful fair," died in childbirth, and Lord Guy "has grown quite gloomy and taciturn," as befits his widowed state.

The story is told in a framework initially set by a stage-direction which identifies the narrator, the time, and the occasion, thereby suggesting also the surroundings and the audience. The phrase "on the night he got his captaincy" gives us the image of a carouse with comrades-in-arms, most likely at an inn, or, as we would say, a pub. This initial assumption is confirmed by the first two lines of the poem quoted above. Twice more during the story we are reminded of the scene of its telling, as the narrator calls for more drink at stanzas nine and fourteen; then we hear no more of it until the ride and the rescue are complete and the narrative has reached its final, ironic climax. At stanza twenty-seven we return from St. Hubert's Chase in the 1640's to the inn of 1660. The speaker comments on growing old, on the fates of his former friends; he hints at the strength of his old, lost love, and concludes with an urgent call for sack and whiskey because, as he has remarked thirty lines earlier, "the more we swallow the less we shall think."

The structure of the story is well managed. The first stanza is introductory. It sets the scene of the storytelling, introduces two names of significance to the story (Miles and Britomarte) and one more (Cuthbert) which belongs only to the framework, and mentions the braid of hair which the narrator carries. The following five stanzas are the exposition, which sets forth the whole situation at St. Hubert's Chase up to the time of Leigh's arrival. Stanzas seven to twelve concern the demand for surrender, the council of war, and the plan for rescue. Stanza thirteen begins the central action, which moves with a continuous rush until the climax of victory at stanza twenty-three, followed by a coda, and a second climax at stanza twenty-six.

It will be noticed that there are two climaxes and they are in two different keys. The first, in the major key, is romantic and triumphant; the second, in the minor, is ironic. The first is direct:

> Though they fought like fiends, we were four to one,
> And we captured those that refused to run.

The second is indirect and understated:

> I sought the hall—where a wedding *had been*—
> The wedding of Guy and of Gwendoline.

The reward which conventional romance grants to the hero is withheld. Not only so, but the extra effort which the hero had put forth is the cause of its withholding. It was while he lay unconscious, recovering from his wound, that Lord Guy won and wed Gwendoline—and he need not have been unconscious for so long. He had collapsed because he had insisted, against the advice of Lord Guy, on riding back with the rescue party and sharing in the final fight. It was a needless gesture and it seems to have cost him the lady.

These thoughts lead to another question: how much of Gordon is in the poem and how much of Jane Bridges is in Gwendoline? Leigh clearly is in love with Gwendoline; she is not clearly in love with him. His social standing is ambiguous. He is evidently

the illegitimate son of a nobleman who was a friend of Gwendoline's mother. He was sergeant, not captain, until the Restoration.
He had been Gwendoline's playmate, never her sweetheart. We
ask ourselves, could he have become her lover and husband if he
had made the effort? Was it from necessity or choice that he
played Sidney Carton, without the fatal ending, to Gwendoline's
Lucie Darnay? There are two parallels in all this with the affair
of Jane Bridges. First, although Gordon's birth was incomparably
better than hers, he had "stained his pedigree" and must have
had either a sense of unworthiness or a lively fear that she or
her family might think him unworthy. Secondly, neither Gordon
nor Ralph Leigh declared his feelings in time.

Much else in the poem is characteristic of Gordon. Many
readers and commentators have noted that here, as in other
poems, it is Gordon the horseman that we are hearing. The
heart of the poem is the ride out of the castle and across country
to Westbrooke. We feel here the accents of a man who loves
good horses and who knows what it is to ride them. There is
something else, too. In the third-to-last stanza he sums up the
whole issue of the Civil War:

> They fought like fiends (give the fiend his due)—
> We fought like fops, it was thus they won.

This is not only characteristic of Gordon, the professional steeple-
chaser; it is characteristically Australian. A recurrent theme in
Australian poetry of the late nineteeth century is the theme of
professional competence, unpretentious and unfoppish. A. B.
Paterson's "The Man from Snowy River" presents the theme, and
"Tom Collins" labors the contrast between the gentlemanly, ama-
teurish, new-chum and the native Australian who knows his job.[1]
In a once familiar poem by Sir Henry Newbolt, which happens
to be called "The Gay Gordons," we read that the Colonel is
happy in midst of battle because

> He sees his work and he sees the way,
> He knows his time and the word to say.[2]

This is the same notion, with a difference. It is un-Australian in
two ways. In an Australian poem it would most likely be the
private, or at most the N. C. O., who would be pictured as on
top of his work; and, secondly, he would not be especially happy
about it, but merely getting on with it.

There is still more of Gordon in the poem, in its mood of wry acceptance of life. Ralph Leigh looks to the past when he was vigorous, and contrasts it with the present, when "pulses beat slow" and "blood runs cold" and "loves have flown." He now lives only for the evenings when lamps are lighted and drinks go round. This was not Gordon's method of reconciling himself to fate, but it was close to the spirit of his later years.

The poem called "Unshriven" is obviously derived from the style of the Old Ballads. It is in four-line stanzas, rhythmically comparable to the conventional ballad-meter. The narrative is elliptical, much of it expressed in conversation. Diction is archaic. The story evidently belongs to the sixteenth century, or earlier, and is one of unexplained violence.

Ellipsis is prominent in the ballad tradition, "Bonnie George Campbell" being a good example.

> He saddled, he bridled,
> and gallant rode he,
> And hame cam his guid horse,
> but never cam he.[3]

We do not know why he rode out, nor what happened to him. Almost the whole story is left to the reader's imagination.

This is what Gordon does in "Unshriven." He gives us the bare bones of the story, and that is all. The knight, known only as "he," rides out on the morning after his wedding. He has killed someone, it would appear, so recently that he has not yet confessed and been absolved. He goes out to keep some sort of appointment, probably with the "avenger" seeking "retribution" for his earlier deed. He departs, over the protest of his bride, and is killed. We are not told who it was that he had killed earlier, or why, or what were the circumstances of his marriage, or what point of honour compelled him to ride out upon the moor on the day after his wedding, or how he was killed. Was he ambushed, or was he treacherously outnumbered, or had he overestimated his own strength and skill? All these details are left to the imagination of the reader in the manner of the Old Ballads.

The versification is peculiarly interesting. The conventional meter of the ballads is that of a four-line stanza, with four stresses in the first and third lines and three in the second and fourth. If a rigid pattern were observed, the lines would have eight and six syllables, respectively. The lines of "Unshriven" are a good deal longer, and if they were treated in the usual way, the scansion would work out something like this:

```
    x   /  │x    /    │x    /   │ x   x    / │x   /   │/x   /
My arm │ is strong, │ I ween, │ and my trus│ty blade │ is keen,
    x    x    /  │x   /  │ x   /  │x    /   │ x     /
And the cours│er that │ I ride │ is swift │ and sure.
```

In stresses, the rhythm is in sixes and fives; in syllables, it is
thirteen and eleven for these particular lines. But we need not
read the lines in this way. We could read them instead as:

```
        x    /   x   //   x   /     x   x   /  x  //   x   /
    My arm is strong, I ween, and my trusty blade is keen,
          x    x   /   x  x  x  /   x  //   x   /
    And the courser that I ride is swift and sure.
```

Read thus, the lines have four major stresses in the first and
three in the second, with one, two, or three unstressed or
secondarily stressed syllables leading up to each syllable which
carries a main stress. The final lines of the poem show this effect
even more clearly:

```
    x    x   /    x    x  x    /    x    x   / x    x   x        /
For the night rack nestles dark round the body stiff and stark,
    x    x   /  x  x  x   /   x    x   x   /
And unshriven to its Maker flies the soul.
```

As can be seen, each of the long lines is internally rhymed. For
the rhythm, the question is, in which way ought we to read the
poem? The answer is, "either," or "both." It is possible to read
the poem in either fashion while simultaneously conscious of the
alternative pattern. Most readers will probably read it in the
rhythm of the Old Ballads, understressing some of the important
syllables to that end.

One line in the poem shows a verbal neatness of which Gordon
was sometimes capable:

Spurr'd and belted, so he rode, steel to draw and steel to goad.

The imagery of the two kinds of steel, the specific word "spurr'd"
coupled with the suggestive word "belted," the repetitive effect
of the two phrases in the second half of the line—all combine to
make an effective image. Even the chiasmus, though it may have
been dictated by the rhyme, adds to the effect.

From these two poems we turn to "Fauconshawe," a less happy
example of Gordon's old-world narrative. Subtitled "A Ballad,"

it tells another story of knights, ladies, and murder, in thirty-one stanzas of six lines each.

Fauconshawe is a castle. The story begins when "little maid Margaret," going to fetch water from the stream near the castle, finds the body of a slain man lying on the brink of the stream. She reports the discovery to the Lady Mabel, who in turn summons Sir Hugh de Vere, her fiancé of long standing, who is at the time a guest in the castle. A crowd of guests and servants goes out to investigate. Sir Hugh recognizes the body as that of an enemy of his own, but an enemy whom he has always respected. He finds in the body a broken dagger. It is clear that the man had not been killed in a fair fight, and that his death is murder. Sir Hugh pronounces a curse on the killer, at which the Lady Mabel turns red and then pale. During the night, the maid Margaret brings to Sir Hugh evidence that it is the Lady Mabel who is guilty; the "murder weapon," as we would call it, belonged to her, and a note of assignation in her handwriting has been found by the body. Sir Hugh goes at midnight to the room in the western tower, where the lady kneels by the dead body. He tells her, somewhat unreasonably, that he does not know or care about the guilt that may lie between her and the dead man, that he will not ask her to declare her innocence, that he does not condemn her, and that he is going to break with her and leave the country. She replies, in the manner of modern diplomacy, that she will neither confirm nor deny his suspicions. He leaves the country, and nothing further is known of either him or the lady.

Like "Unshriven," this poem is in the manner of the Old Ballads. The type of character, the setting both in time and in space, the quality of violence, the use of conversation and the narrative ellipses all combine to this end. The six-line stanza is the ballad meter, with two lines added. The first, third, and fifth lines are tetrameters, and the others trimeters. Counting by syllables, we find that almost every line is longer than the standard pattern of the ballads. Gordon's free mixture of anapaests and iambs gives the verse much of its liveliness and vigour.

There are faults in some places, as if Gordon's ear had failed him. The most striking is at the end of the second-last stanza:

> Unflinchingly she spoke in reply—
> "Go hence with the break of morn,
> "I will neither confess, nor yet deny,
> "I will return thee scorn for scorn."

It is hard to see how the last line can be read metrically, music-ally, poetically, or in any other way than as an awkward chunk of prose that has somehow got mixed up with the verse. The remedy seems simple. To make the line read either "I return thee scorn for scorn," or else "But return thee scorn for scorn," would not only improve it metrically but strengthen the sense as well. Again, in the twenty-second stanza we find "The knight in silence the letter read, / Oh! the characters well he knew." The word "Oh!" does harm. It weakens the rhythm. Besides, though ar-chaism of diction is appropriate to the style, this particular sample is obtrusive and enfeebling. There are other awkward lines in the poem; it does not move with the easy vigor that Gordon achieves elsewhere.

"The Three Friends," subtitled "From the French," is in the same stanza form as "Fauconshawe" but with a different rhythm. With a few exceptions, such as a shortened line at the beginning of the fourth stanza, the lines are regular iambic tetrameter and iambic trimeter, with eight and six syllables each. Variety comes more from the interplay of vowels and consonants than from prosodic irregularities.

The story can be briefly outlined. The narrator is dying, "self-slain by the knife," and speaking to a father-confessor. Three friends had fallen in love with one girl. There followed a deadly elimination contest. The narrator killed one of his friends in a duel in the morning. He met the second at evening over two cups of wine, one being poisoned. The choice of wine-cups was by lot. Both men drank; the narrator lived and the friend died. The survivor went to meet the girl on the following morning. The climax of the story is in the third-last stanza:

> She fled! I cannot prove her guilt,
> Nor would I an I could;
> See, life for life is fairly spilt!
> And blood is shed for blood;
> Her white hands neither touched the hilt,
> Nor yet the potion brew'd.

Once more we have the gap in the story. Why did she flee? What was the "guilt" that the narrator cannot prove? In what way was she responsible for the three deaths? Was it merely that her beauty was a snare, or was there something more concrete? The imagination has not quite enough to work on, and the story leaves us not quite satisfied.

"Rippling Water" is not so much a story as a narrative situa-

tion. The "maiden" is going to be married to Marmaduke, but
has doubts about the choice. Marmaduke has "wealth and power
and rank and pride." Stephen, who lives in a cottage and "works
for his daily bread," once loved her and planned to marry her,
and she had been in love with him, but "that was long ago." Old
Giles, the gardener, is not easy about the marriage. He hopes that
Marmaduke will be kinder to her than he had been to Giles and
his family in their need. Blind Dame Martha, credited with
second sight, has remarked in sinister fashion that "useless warn-
ings are scarcely kind." Brian of Hawkesmede, noble but poor,
has given her to understand that Marmaduke is a coward. But
she has made her choice, and it is against both Stephen and
Brian.

> Stephen must toil a living to gain,
> Plough and harrow and gather the grain;
> Brian has little enough to maintain
>   The station in life he needs must fill;
> Both are fearless and kind and frank,
>   But we can't have all gifts under the sun—
> What have I won save riches and rank?
> (The rippling water murmurs on).

We learn in the last stanza what we have suspected from the
beginning, that she is a "peasant girl." She is irresistibly attracted
by wealth and what goes with it, even while she asks:

> But the love of one that I cannot love,
>   Will it last when the gloss of his toy is gone?

The poem is in seven stanzas of twelve lines each, with a close-
knit rhyme-scheme, *a b a b a a a b c d c d*. A refrain-line "(The
rippling water murmurs on)," recurs as the second and the last
line of each stanza, which adds to the ballad-like impression.
The structure is well balanced, the lines smooth, and even the
characterization adequate for the purpose.

Once again we ask: Have we in the poem an echo of Jane
Bridges? It would not be unreasonable to suppose so, though it
might be unjust. As we have seen in Chapter I, Jane had sufficient reason for refusing Gordon; we need not suppose, as some
have done, that she was simply determined to marry money.
But Gordon might have come to think that she had, especially
in retrospect, years later. If there was a connection, it was likely
an unconscious one.

If we are to seek for these deep-hid parallels, there is one to

be found, or invented, in "A Legend of Madrid." The story is told
in alternating soliloquies by Francesca and Nina, who are watching a bull-fight. Francesca is a "proud and high-born lady, /
Daughter of an ancient race." She had fallen in love with the
matador, and had promised to marry him. Then, he had changed
his mind and had married, instead, Nina, "the muleteer's child."
Now both women are watching the bull-fight, the one anxious
for her husband's safety and the other hot for vengeance and
eager to see him killed. The matador kills the first bull and Nina
is in ecstacy. Then the second bull comes out, the "famed Cor-
dovan beast." This time it is the matador who is killed, and
Francesca triumphs. The poem ends with Francesca speaking:

> Through the doublet, torn and riven,
>   Where the stunted horn was driven,
> Wells the life-blood—We are even,
>   Daughter of the muleteer!

It is tempting, albeit far-fetched, to see in this a parallel to the
two women in Gordon's life. It is true that Jane was better born
than Maggie, though, strictly speaking, not by much. It is true
also that it was Maggie that he married. On the other side, we
remember that he did not desert Jane; she refused him and is
not known to have had any regrets afterward. But if she had
had them, she would have been well avenged by the later course
of Gordon's life, his marriage, and the manner of his end. For the
purposes of poetry, where any element may be transposed into
its opposite, the parallel is enough to be significant. Theories of
comparative religion have been built on foundations no stronger.

We have kept to the last of this group one poem which some
readers have thought to be Gordon's finest in its kind, "The
Rhyme of Joyous Garde."[4] It is a reminiscent soliloquy by Lancelot, toward the end of his life. As a narrative, it is a compressed
review of the central Arthurian story, opening with a landscape
description of a fine spring day, in contrast with the mood of the
speaker. There follows a sketch of the early comradeship with
King Arthur, the mission to bring Guinevere, "A bride to a
queenly bridal," the beginning and the growth of guilty love, the
scandal, the king's trust, the siege of Joyous Garde, and the final
"crime of Modred." The fate of Guinevere, now dead, is revealed
by two separated lines: the first, "She had leisure for shame and
sorrow—," and the second, spoken about her golden hair, "Was
it shorn when the church vows bound her?"

Intermingled with the rest there are vivid miniature battle-pieces, such as the eighth stanza:

> But I strove full grimly beneath his weight,
> I clung to his poignard desperate,
>   I baffled the thrust that followed,
> And writhing uppermost rose, to deal,
> With bare three inches of broken steel,
> One stroke—Ha! the headpiece crash'd piecemeal,
>   And the knave in his black blood wallow'd.

What is important is not the story, which most readers know already, but the characterization. We see Lancelot in repentance. It is a Lancelot with whom we can sympathize. His love for Guinevere, though illicit, is brought to our imagination as human and genuine, yet not sentimentalized as Guinevere's was, however persuasively, by William Morris in "The Defence of Guenevere." Arthur comes out better than in Tennyson's *The Idylls of the King*. He is possibly more gullible, but at the same time more human, more manly, and less of a symbol. The ending is an expression of hope, hope that through repentance and forgiveness there may be a transmutation of evil to good,

> When the world as a wither'd leaf shall be,
> And the sky like a shrivell'd scroll shall flee,
> And souls shall be summon'd from land and sea,
>   At the blast of His bright archangel.

The form is stanzaic. It is a seven-line stanza, rhyming *a a b c c c b*. The *b* lines have three stresses, the others four. The *b* rhymes are feminine throughout. Within the lines, the rhythms are compounded of Gordon's characteristic blending of the iambic and the anapaestic, the ends of the lines being regularly iambic.

The poem can hardly be denied substantial merit. It is a capsule version of the Arthurian story, and an imaginative insight into the emotions of a re-created character. The lines are vigorous and often musical. This may not be great poetry, but it is verse of a very high order.

II *Stories from the Present*

We come now to the narratives which belonged not to a historic or legendary past, but to Gordon's own age. Of all his narrative poems, the most popular was "How We Beat the

Favourite." It is a straightforward story of a steeplechase with a close finish. The English setting is admitted by the subtitle, "A Lay of the Loamshire Hunt Cup," but in the poem itself there is nothing in the spirit and little in the detail that hinders us from feeling it as an Australian yarn.

The speaker, the "squire," is to ride Iseult. The favorite is The Clown, ridden by Dick Neville. Our sympathies are enlisted against the favorite at the beginning, by a suggestion of some hanky-panky in The Clown's entry. Dick Neville calls himself a "gentleman rider," but the claim is scouted. (". . . if he's a gent who the mischief's a jock?"). The horse likewise would be ineligible if the rules were properly enforced. The race is for *bona fide* hunters, which The Clown is not. But Dick Neville has influential connections, and the steward turns a blind eye.

"Down went the flag." The race is on. Iseult is well back at first, but after nine jumps have taken their toll, the mare flies out in front. Just after the turn for home, The Clown makes his challenge, and pulls a length in front. They come even again and at one jump there is a clash of stirrups. They diverge, The Clown gets the shorter route, and again is ahead; but again Iseult pulls even. From here on it is neck-and-neck running, with Dick Neville's whip going and the crowd roaring.

> Aye! so ends the tussle,—I knew the tan muzzle
> Was first, though the ring-men were yelling "Dead heat!"
> A nose I could swear by, but Clarke said, "The mare by
> A short head." And that's how the favourite was beat.

The verse is lively, basically anapaestic. The four-line stanzas are rhymed *a b a b*, but there is internal rhyme in the first and third lines, and these are feminine rhymes throughout. In versification, the poem is a minor *tour de force*.

There is little that is apparent of formal narrative structure, but there is more than appears to the casual eye. There are nine stanzas of introduction, which not only introduce the *dramatis personae* but direct our sympathies and create an atmosphere. Then the race begins, and there is a well-managed "build" of the tension which reaches its climax at the end of stanza twenty-one, with the words "lock'd level the hurdles we flew." This is followed by three stanzas of blur and uncertainty ("All sights seen obscurely, all shouts vaguely heard") which ends with "flits the white post." The final four lines gives us the result, with a neat touch of contrapuntal imagery of the shouting "ring-men" against the authoritative certainty of the "squire" and Clarke.

"Banker's Dream" is an earlier and much slighter piece in the same vein. It was one of the "Hippodromania" series of rhymed predictions, or comments, concerning coming races. It tells the story of a steeplechase, all but the finish. The speaker is awakened just before the end of the race.

There is a letter from Gordon to William Trainor, printed in the *Reminiscences and Unpublished Pieces,* which describes the course and tactics of a race, the relevant paragraph beginning "The race was run in this way. I got the lead. . . ."[5] Among the horses mentioned are Banker, Cadger, and Echo (the winner). It has been supposed that Gordon had this race in mind when he wrote "Banker's Dream," but the dates are against that supposition. "Banker's Dream" was published in *Bell's Life* on April 20, 1867; the letter is dated the following October.

Unlike "How We Beat the Favourite," "Banker's Dream" is entirely Australian, and its story, whatever its origin, is close to Gordon's own experiences. Two of his own best-known horses are mentioned, Cadger and Ingleside. In style the poem is less satisfactory. It has vigor, but it lacks the metrical finish of "How We Beat the Favourite" and may with reason be thought of as a trial run for the later poem.

We come now to two poems which differ from the rest and which have some kinship with each other. Both are Australian stories, of Gordon's own time. Both are serious stories, involving matters of life and death. Both are stories of out-of-door, adventurous exploits. And both have been erroneously accepted as poetical versions of Gordon's own experience.

The first of these is "From the Wreck," the fourth poem in *Bush Ballads and Galloping Rhymes.* It may well have been suggested by what happened on the coast of Gordon's own part of Australia, in 1859. At five o'clock on a Saturday afternoon in early August (which is deep winter in southern Australia) the *Admella,* a ship of three hundred and sixty tons, struck side-on to a reef, a mile-and-half from the shore, about twenty miles north of Cape Northumberland. Within a quarter of an hour she broke into three parts. The central section sank at once. The fore and aft sections were heeled over and the survivors could do little but cling to rails and rigging, cold, wet, and hungry. The seas were high, the ship's boats were soon crushed, adrift, or unserviceable, and four men were drowned in attempts to get ashore and summon help. It was clear that help was not going to come by itself. The shore was deserted, and there seemed no chance of their being sighted from the water. On the Sunday afternoon, John Leach and Robert Knapman succeeded in getting ashore, after a long, cold, and exhausting swim. It was seven o'clock on the following morning when they reached the light-house at Cape Northumberland. The lightkeeper reached the Mount Gambier telegraph station eight hours later, and had messages sent to Melbourne and Adelaide. Boats were then dis-patched to the rescue, but it was not until the following Saturday morning that the survivors, twenty-one men and one woman out of a total complement of one hundred and thirteen, were finally taken off the ship.

Out of this event, which he would surely have heard of during his time at Dingley Dell, if not earlier, Gordon made his poem. In his version, two men make the ride. Jack, the speaker, is on a young, finely bred mare; Alec, evidently an older man familiar with the countryside and the "near cuts" ("short cuts" in Amer-ican nomenclature), rides a heavier black horse named "Boling-broke." Their function is to "Ride straight with the news—they may send some relief / From the township and we—we can do little more."- After "bridling with hurry, and saddling with haste," they ride out into the pre-dawn blackness, among trees and across a range. In dawn light they get across a flooded creek and into the scrub beyond it. When they get into open country they make a race of it. Near the end of the journey, Alec drops out, leaving Jack, a lighter man on a younger, fresher horse, to finish the ride. Once within the township, the mare staggers, chokes, and goes down.

> I slipp'd off the bridle, I slackened the girth,
>> I ran on and left her and told them my news;
> I saw her soon afterwards. What was she worth?
>> How much for her hide? She had never worn shoes.

This is how the poem ends, as Gordon printed it in 1870. As happened with "The Sick Stockrider," there had been an addi-tional four lines which Gordon finally decided to omit:

> There are songs yet unsung, there are tales yet untold
>> Concerning yon wreck that must baffle my pen;
> Let Kendall write legends in letters of gold,
>> Of deeds done and known among children of men.[6]

Few today will dispute his judgment. The ending of the poem as we now have it, in its abruptness and ironic pathos, is stronger than the graceful but irrelevant reference to Kendall.

A legend long persisted that Gordon had taken part in this
ride. His widow said so, in 1912.[7] Harry Stockdale said so, in
some penciled notes which he set down in 1923.[8] But it cannot
be so, in view of the circumstantial account to be found in the
South Australian archives, and the fuller published account by
Mossman. Further detail is added by A. T. Saunders, whose account[9] is apparently based on a parliamentary paper of 1859.
According to this information, the head light-keeper at Cape
Northumberland was Ben Germain. His horse had been missing
for weeks. When the men from *Admella* reached the lighthouse,
he borrowed a horse from Mr. Black's station nearby, but it
threw him after a couple of miles, and the actual ride was made
by young Black, the station-owner's son. Gordon's name does
not appear in any of these records, nor is there any evidence that
he was in the vicinity at the time.

The story of "Wolf and Hound" is related to Gordon's life in
much the same way as the poem just considered. It is a police
story, and therefore, because Gordon was for two years a policeman, some readers have supposed that he took part in the incident narrated. There is no evidence to support that notion, and
it is on the face of it most unlikely.

The speaker is, or has been, a mounted policeman; he is recall-
ing an occasion on which he was in pursuit of a criminal. He
had set out with two others, M'Crea and Young Marsden, and
had left them behind when their horses played out. His own
beast went lame with a flint in her shoe. At the cost of some
delay, he removed the stone, but he had lost the trail of his
quarry, and there was nothing to do but head for Hawthorndell
and hope that he might get there. He threw the reins on his
mare's neck, and was carried to the Warrigal water springs. By
the water's edge he saw footprints of both horse and man. His
man had surely been there. On looking around, he felt equally
sure that the outlaw had gone into the cavern in a rock wall
close by. After looking to his revolver and removing his shoes,
he crept to the mouth of the cave and crawled inside. Suddenly,
both the silence and the darkness were broken by a pistol shot,
which missed. An exchange of shots followed. The outlaw had
the advantage, as he was shooting toward the light, whereas his
opponent was aiming into the darkness, guided only by pistol-
flashes. One ball grazed the policeman's ear. A couple of shots
later, another broke his right arm. He struck out blindly with
his left hand, and found that his last shot had killed his man.
"I had shot him dead in his den." So the poem ends.

This one requires little comment. It is ninety-six lines, and although not printed in stanzas but in sections of varying length, it is in fact in ballad-meter, with alternating four-beat and three-beat lines, and with alternate rhyme. It is not a story so much as a versified incident, although it does have a plot that would be patient of analysis and it ends in the sudden climax that Gordon favored. The idea that Gordon himself ever had such an experience or performed such a feat is as irrelevant as it is unlikely.

There is a poem which holds a special place among Gordon's narratives. "The Roll of the Kettledrum; or, The Lay of the Last Charger" is the final, climactic piece in *Sea Spray and Smoke Drift*. The speaker is a horse which had taken part, years earlier, in the Charge of the Light Brigade at Balaclava. The poem itself does not name the action, but it is clear partly from the imagery of the poem itself and partly from external evidence that that is what is meant. The story of the charge is vividly told, with such touches as "Thrusting his hand in his breast or breast pocket, / While from his wrist the sword swung by a chain." The horse's rider was killed at the very end of the action.

The story of the charge takes up less than half of the poem. The rest is a somewhat rambling soliloquy, with two main topics. One is the praise of the horse and the pride of horse-hood. The other is the sad passage of time, as symbolized by the figure of the "gallant old colonel," who

> came limping and halting,
> The day before yesterday, into my stall;
> Oh! light to the saddle I've once seen him vaulting,
> In full marching order, steel broadsword and all.

Indeed, it is a dichotomous poem. The first part seems to set a theme of action and of courage, but in the end it turns out to be a poem in praise of death.

III *Summary*

We have now examined each of Gordon's major narratives, with three noteworthy exceptions. "The Sick Stockrider," though partly narrative, has more in it of reminiscence and meditation, and is better left for treatment in other connections. *The Feud* requires, for other reasons, separate consideration.

The ballads and narratives have been praised, and indeed they have been overpraised, but not without some reason. It may seem absurd to compare Gordon with Tennyson to the disadvantage of the latter. Nevertheless, Gordon's lines on the Charge of the Light Brigade have an immediacy that Tennyson does not achieve, nor attempt. F. W. L. Adams stated the point with exemplary neatness when he wrote, in 1886, that Tennyson "watched his charge through Mr. Russell's field-glasses, and we follow his view of it, but Gordon has ridden it and takes us with him."[10] This is Gordon's great strength. He writes, not so much of his experience, but out of his experience, and especially in his ballads of action and of horsemanship.

As a rule his stories are well constructed. Sometimes he over-does the elliptical quality of the ballads, so that the reader feels an awkward gap in the sense. Mostly, though, we are carried along by the rush of the verse and the *élan* with which the story is presented. This is mainly true in the modern stories. When writing in the vein of the Old Ballads he uses a more deliberate tempo. The two effects are related somewhat as a series of still-pictures is related to a motion picture.

There is a weakness in characterization. In a brief narrative one does not expect much vividness or complexity in the exploration of characters, but we may hope for more than Gordon ordinarily gives us. The persons in Gordon's narratives seldom come to life in our imagination. Browning's Pied Piper and his Mayor of Hamelin have more reality than "Jack" and "Alec" of "From the Wreck." In "The Rhyme of Joyous Garde" Gordon has some success in bringing his persons to life, but this is exceptional.

What is important is that he gives us storytelling verse. Fiction is a fundamental need; all else in literature is luxury-goods by comparison. Since Chaucer, the narrative has been the weakest strand in English poetry,[11] and it is especially weak in the "colonial" literatures of the mid-nineteenth century. That it is stronger in the Australian than in the Canadian poetry of the period is partly to the credit of Adam Lindsay Gordon.

CHAPTER 4

Two Special Narratives

BECAUSE of its length and complexity, *Ashtaroth* needs separate consideration, distinct from the more compact story-poems of the better-known volumes. But before we come to discuss Gordon's long, involved "dramatic lyric," we shall consider another narrative poem which also stands apart from the others.

I *"The Feud"*

The Feud tells an old familiar tale which is also a useful example of the tragic pattern sometimes called the "epic conflict" —more accurately, the "epic dilemma." The feud involves two families, the daughter of one being married to a son of the other. From the woman's standpoint, no matter who wins, she must be a loser. This narrative pattern is at least as old as the Old English fragment of "The Fight at Finnsburg" and the "Finnsburg Lay" in *Beowulf*.[1] The particular example with which Gordon is concerned is the Old Ballad known by various titles, as "The Braes of Yarrow," or "The Dowie Dens of Yarrow."

Gordon built his poem from two sources. One was his memory of the ballad itself, and the other was the set of engravings from Noel Paton's six paintings. The shape of the poem is thus imposed by the engravings; it is in six parts, headed "Plate I," "Plate II," and so on. The result is a series of scenes that present the story in a theatrical sequence.

"Plate I," subtitled "Rixa super mero," is the scene of the quarrel. The first half of the last stanza, "They've settled the time and they've settled the place, / They've paid for the wine and the ale," parallels vividly enough the opening of the earlier traditional version, but with a small difference. One version of the Ballad begins:

> Late at e'en, drinking the wine,
> And ere they paid the lawing,
> They set a combat them between,
> To fight it in the dawing.[2]

This version is found in a collection of poems edited for schools, and it differs from those collected by F. J. Child.[3] Nevertheless, it is likely to be nearer to the version that Gordon had once known; in any event he was bound by the content of the picture.

"Plate II" deals with the farewell between the hero and his bride. There is one significant difference from the earlier version. Instead of the realistic foresight of "My cruel brother will you betray," Gordon assigns to the bride a premonition based on a dream. In "Plate III" she is waiting, oppressed by uneasiness, restlessness, and foreboding. At the end of the section she rides off toward Yarrow, with her elder sister and a moss-trooper, bent on finding out what has happened. "Plate IV" tells the story of the fight, in which both principals are killed. "Plate V," the longest section, begins with the coming of "the traitor's father" to the glen. As he surveys the bodies, his widowed daughter arrives. He recapitulates the events that have led up to the struggle, tries to console his daughter, and urges her to "Forget the deed! and learn to call / A worthier man your lord." She repudiates the notion, and presently, "stretched upon the dead man's breast / With one long weary sigh," she dies. "Plate VI" is the funeral, not narrated but suggested in what is really eight lines of ballad-meter, printed as four long lines.

There is some merit in this early work. The story is made vivid, more vivid in some respects than the original version. The immediate cause of the quarrel is not left vague. The bridegroom claims the land which had been promised to him as a dowry. The brother, repudiating his father's pledge, demands that the bridegroom resign his claim. The story of the fight is told with added detail. Greater prominence is given to the plight, the feelings, the actions, and the words of the bride, who is the emotional focus of the story. Lastly, the flexible use of the ballad rhythm is strikingly successful. Gordon already displays his characteristic mingling of iambic and anapaestic feet, using strictly iambic lines to slow the rhythm in the second half of the poem. The rhyme-scheme is *a b a b* (unlike the traditional *a b c b* pattern of the Old Ballads) varied by an occasional six-line stanza rhymed *a b a b a b*. The final section, "Plate VI," subtitled "Dies irae: dies illa," is printed in long lines skillfully slowed down by the use of long vowels, stopped consonants, internal rhyme, and a feminine rhyme at the very close.

II   *Ashtaroth*

Ashtaroth is a horse of a very different color. Many readers must have wondered why it was ever written, and even more must have wondered why it was ever published. It has been generally deprecated and disregarded. Writing in the *Melbourne Review* (VIII, 438 f.), Alexander Sutherland suggested that when the story has been mastered the details of the poem can be enjoyed. It would seem, therefore, useful to try to sort out the storyline of the poem, but it will not be easy.[4]

There are thirty-one scenes in the whole work. These are not numbered, but are merely indicated by successive headings, as "SCENE—A CASTLE IN NORMANDY," or "SCENE—THE SAME." This is not a poetic drama, but a dramatic poem, well sprinkled with "songs" in a manner reminiscent of early musical comedy without chorus. But this is no comedy.

We are introduced to the protagonist at once. Hugo, a Norman baron, excuses himself from a feast that is ready to begin. He wishes to stay in his tower-study, with his books, star-maps, and astronomical instruments. There is a second person with him, named "Orion." Orion seems to be suggesting that Hugo's studies are both futile and inept, and that he would do better to pursue power or pleasure. Orion sings Hugo to sleep with verses to this effect. At daybreak, when Hugo wakes, the conversation is continued. (Scene ii.) Orion offers a short-cut to the knowledge that Hugo wants, and reminds him that he has "prosper'd much" since the day when, a "landless knight," he first met Orion. But Hugo shies away from this new offer, asserting that "There is now no compact between us twain." He decides to go on a journey, starting "this very day," in order to "quiet this restless soul." The third scene is a soliloquy of one hundred and fifty-two lines, spoken by Hugo on a Breton sea-cliff, expressing the melancholy puzzlement which his search for knowledge has brought him.

Scene iv, back in Hugo's castle, introduces new characters and further information, some of it very important. It begins with "Thora's Song" ("We severed in autumn early"), a lyric of loneliness which was to be reprinted in *Bush Ballads and Galloping Rhymes*. Thora is evidently Hugo's wife, and she is talking with Elspeth, her nurse. We hear of her two sisters, married to Max and to Biorn respectively. News comes of Hugo's return. The messenger reports that "little of note has happened" to the travelers; they had only been shipwrecked, captured in mistake for pirates, and released.

Next, a Danish knight named "Harold" appears and is recognized as a foe of Hugo's. He brings a letter to Hugo, hands it

over, leaves against Thora's protest, and conveniently dies a
couple of scenes later in the presence of the monk, Luke, who
is able to report his last words. It is suggested that death has
been due to exposure; there are references to a wild night and
driving hail.

At this point the story becomes more complicated. The letter
which Harold has brought contains a dying request from Hugo's
old comrade, Baldwin, that he (Hugo) escort Baldwin's daughter
Agatha to the Englemehr convent, on the Rhine. Now, Agatha
was at one time engaged to Hugo, and during the engagement
she tried to elope with Harold, who had been married to (but
was then separated from) Hugo's sister, Dorothea. Hugo had
overtaken the absconding couple and restored the *status quo*—
or, if we are to be meticulous in our Latin, the *statum quo*.

Scenes x to xiv contain the journey to the convent on the Rhine
and the beginning of Hugo's return home. It is made clear that
he is still in love with Agatha and reluctant to return to Thora.

The next three scenes (xv to xvii) are purely "gothic." Hugo
has reached the Norman frontier. He has been riding all day and
studying all night. Orion suggests a night ride, offers him a
mount and also a beverage containing hellebore, upas, and other
like ingredients. They ride on black horses, through a tempest,
to a mountain peak, where they dismount. Orion conjures up
spirits—obviously evil spirits. Four "shadowy altars" appear. The
first of these "a golden-hued fire shows"; it represents Mammon.
The second is distinguished by "blood-red flame," for Moloch.
The third is "tinged like the rose"; it stands for Ashtaroth, now
to be identified with Astarte. The fourth altar, which shows only
a column of black smoke, is unexplained and unvisited. "With
that," declares Orion, "we have nothing to do." Each of the
three altars is approached in turn. The emphasis is on the third
one, the altar of Ashtaroth. The meaning seems to be that Hugo
is struggling against his passion for Agatha, and that Orion is
encouraging that passion. In the following scene, the eighteenth,
Hugo decides to turn back and ride toward the Rhine once
more; that is, to Agatha. Orion comments, " 'Gainst the logic of
the devil / Human logic strives in vain."

The nineteenth scene introduces an entirely new set of characters, and a new development in the action. In a camp near the
Black Forest, a band of freebooters, under Rudolph of Rothen-
stein, are discussing their problems. They are too few to fight
against the army of Prince Otto, and they need both food and
money. Orion, who appears in disguise as one of the band,
points out that

> There is wealth untold
> In the ancient convent of Englemehr;
> That is not so very far from here.

The decision is made to attack the convent.

From this point the story becomes more complex than ever. Hugo wishes to defend the convent. Orion argues that the monks do not deserve his help, and that the attack will assist him to Agatha. Eric (a friend of Hugo's who had earlier left to visit his mother and who had mysteriously rejoined Hugo's party) goes to try negotiations with Rudolph. Messengers are sent to Prince Otto for help, but at least one of them is captured. The nuns, though offered safe-conduct, refuse to leave the convent. Hugo and his men organize the defense. They beat off the first assault. They feel sure, however, that they will be overwhelmed by the second, especially since, as we now learn, Hugo is dead. At this point, Eric brings word that the forces of Prince Otto are in sight. The convent is now safe, and the poem concludes, somewhat in the manner of *The Feud*, with a funeral dirge.

The foregoing attempt at an extended synopsis has had two purposes. First, if one is to read the poem with any satisfaction, the first requirement, and the first difficulty, is to grasp in some way the bare bones of the plot. Secondly, the summary may give a little notion of why the poem was not well received in 1867, and has not been generally well regarded since.

Let us first consider its faults. As a story it lacks both unity and clarity. Too much is left out, and too much is inserted. There is an exaggeration both of ellipsis and of irrelevancy, and especially the latter. We hear, for example, of Thora's two sisters. Their husbands are named and their marriages are categorized. Then we hear no more of them, and what looks like (in theatrical parlance) a "plant" turns out to be a pointless intrusion of non-significant information. There is a hint of bad feeling between Hugo and an Abbot—of indefinite status and function—at Englemehr, but not enough is made of the fact to justify its inclusion. The purpose of the fourth altar in the apparition-scene (the seventeenth) is left wholly unexplained and the entire scene is muddled. The penultimate scene, the thirtieth, is worse. The reader gets the impression at the beginning of the scene that the first skirmish has gone well for the defenders. Gradually, and ambiguously, he is allowed to know that Hugo's party has suffered crippling losses. Then, almost incidentally, we learn that Hugo is dead. The best we can say of this scene is that the subtlety overreaches itself.

Though interesting characterization is not greatly to be expected in this kind of narrative, we get even less than we have a right to ask for. None of the persons is much more than a symbol or a label. Hugo's dying words do bring in a breath of reality:

"How heavy the night hangs—how wild the waves dash;
Say a mass for my soul—and give Rollo a mash."

There is a wry touch of Gordon himself here, but it is too little and too late. Orion is a vaguely Mephistophelian character. He alone has no descriptive note in the *Dramatis Personae*. He is a tempter and a conjurer, but his purpose is vague, except where he is working to make Hugo yield to his passion for Agatha. Thora and Agatha seem to be contrasted, the one as the epic woman—the faithful wife and partner—and the other as romantic woman—the object of passionate, and unlawful, quest. But none of the characters stands out as a person. This flatness, which we might accept in a ballad, seems a serious lack in a long, dramatic poem.

The style is uneven. Much praise has been given to "Thora's Song," which opens the fourth scene. It is a smooth and pleasant lyric; the alliteration is unobtrusive and seems less than it is; the vowel-play makes it a good poem for reading aloud. It invites comparison with Tennyson's "Mariana," and judged by that comparison it lacks both precision and development of imagery. "The warm sun riseth and setteth, / The night bringeth moistening dew," is pallid beside Tennyson's

When the thick-moted sunbeam lay
Athwart the chambers, and the day
Was sloping toward his western bower.

Gordon's imagery does not give us, as Tennyson's does, the sense of time moving onward. We know that time has passed, but we do not feel it. On the other hand, the simple refrain-line, "Thou comest not back again"—varied in the final stanza to "He cometh not back again"—must be preferred by many readers to the irritating jingle of Tennyson's four-line refrain.

Ashtaroth also contains some of the worst bathos in English poetry. Hugo's comment on Harold the Dane, in the sixth scene, is notorious:

Indeed, I have not the least idea;
The man is certainly mad.
He wedded my sister, Dorothea,
And used her cruelly bad.

There are some lines of Orion's in the seventeenth scene which
are not much better:

> There are subjects on which I dare not touch;
> And if I were to try and enlighten you
> I should probably fail, and possibly frighten you.

These are flat passages. Others are overly intense and artificial.
The deliberate archaism of the whole poem makes it unreal and
distasteful to many.

There are occasional flashes of Gordon's acuteness in catching
the feel of an action. Agatha's tale of her elopement, in Scene xxi,
contains these lines:

> I heard the clash of each warded blow,
>   The click of each parried thrust,
> And the shuffling feet that bruis'd the lawn
>   As they traversed here and there,
> And the breath through the clench'd teeth heavily drawn,
>   When breath there was none to spare.

But these are infrequent. Little that is memorable, except for its
weaknesses, comes to light in this poem.

Much has been made of its imitative qualities. Unfavorable
critics have attacked it as a plagiarism of Goethe's *Faust*. This
seems an exaggeration. The relationship between Hugo and Orion
is roughly analogous to that between Faust and Mephistopheles,
but only roughly. The Faust-theme is, after all, widely known,
and there are other influences more evident. There is the atmosphere of the Gothic novels of the pre-Romantic age. Despite the
dissimilarity in content, *Ashtaroth* seems nearer to "Monk" Lewis
than to Goethe, and nearer to the Byron of *Manfred* than to
either.

And yet, all things considered, it is still the work of a poet—not
of a great poet, and certainly of a poet still in the stage of ap-
prenticeship. Gordon was technically uneducated; as a poet he
was self-taught and self-trained. A long poem of this kind was
beyond his powers. Indeed, any poem of this kind was, in 1867,
two generations out of fashion. The best and the worst that
we can say of it is that a reader who gives it patient attention will find that in spite of its faults it deserves just a little
better than the reprobation it has generally met with.

CHAPTER 5

Reflective Poetry; Gordon and the Age

I *The Poets of the Times*

POETRY expresses the thought of its age, and not only in the
work of the so-called philosophical poets. Any great poet is a
medium for the characteristic ideas, and the fundamental assumptions, of the culture to which he belongs. Homer gives us
a look into the ethics and the theological images of the early
Greeks. We turn to Dante for the essence of the medieval cosmos, to Milton for that of the Puritan seventeenth century, and
to Eliot for the bewilderment of our own times. Not only the
major poets, but the minor ones and even the poetasters enable
us to possess the spirit of an age. Not only Whitman, and Sand-
burg, and Robert Frost, but also James Whitcomb Riley and
Edgar A. Guest reveal the complexities and simplicities of the
American democracy.

Gordon was born in the year of the first Reformed Parliament,
which some historians take as the real beginning of the Victorian Age. His lifetime spanned the years of the Oxford Movement, and of *The Origin of Species*. They were the years when
Victorian Evangelicalism was dominant and also when it was
beginning to crumble. Samuel Butler's *The Evidence for the Res-
urrection of Jesus Christ . . . Critically Examined* appeared anon-
ymously five years before Gordon's death, as did J. R. Seeley's
Ecce Homo. Within his lifetime the conflict between science and
religion, slightly misconceived as a conflict between faith and
reason, had reached its height.

The poets of the time were in the midst of the conflict. In 1850,
three years before Gordon left England, Tennyson's *In Memoriam* burst upon the world which, in part, received it as a reasoned poetic apologia for the superior claim of faith. Tennyson
anticipated the difficulties of Darwinism by nearly a decade. He
saw the anomaly that was to be implicit in the Darwinian view,

as T. H. Huxley was to see it later at the end of his career. Acceptance of a purely materialistic universe would mean in the end the surrender of human values. The same lesson was enforced in *The Lotos-Eaters*, if we take the lotos as a symbol of philosophic materialism which leads to *accidia* and the abandonment of moral effort. In short, Tennyson saw that those who welcomed Darwin in the name of humanism were cutting the ground from under their own feet. Browning wrestled with similar problems in "Christmas Eve," "A Death in the Desert," "Bishop Blougram's Apology," and in Book X of *The Ring and the Book*. Matthew Arnold, in "Dover Beach" and "Stanzas from the Grande Chartreuse," provides the central poetic statement of the negativism of the age. "Dover Beach" confirms Tennyson's earlier prevision that the disappearance of faith would mean also the disappearance of the humane values. Not only are love, joy, and peace not to be found, but by a final irony even significant knowledge is no longer attainable "on a darkling plain, / Where ignorant armies clash by night." At the same time, the lesser poets were dealing with the same questions. A. H. Clough put his doubts, half-beliefs, and vacillations into quiet and sometimes oblique verse, as in "Where Lies the Land" and "Qui Laborat, Orat." Swinburne attacked Christian dogmas and Christian values alike. He and Meredith, in "Hertha" and "The Woods of Westermain" respectively, tried to formulate an alternative religion of nature. Francis Thompson, on the other side, made out of the pivotal religious experience his best-known poem, "The Hound of Heaven."

For many reasons, Gordon was isolated from this fermentation in thought and art. To begin with, his early development was markedly provincial. His education was incomplete. He did not come into touch with the ideas of his time. His vital contacts were with boxers, horse-trainers, and farmers. In a letter of January 13, 1852, he mentions having heard a very good sermon, and indicates an intention to begin going to Sunday school.[1] Evidence that he actually went is lacking. Keble, Newman, Colenso, Strauss—these belonged mainly to a distant and irrelevant world. The migration to Australia aggravated the condition. This was not solely a matter of distance; there were two other factors. One was an anti-intellectual tradition which, though less than sometimes supposed, did exist in Australia as it existed in Canada and over much of the U.S.A. The pioneer community often excuses itself from thinking, on the ground that it needs all its energies for physical survival and economic development. Admittedly it does not greatly differ in this from Thomas Hardy's Wessex, for example; but in Australia in the mid-nineteenth century there was not only a lack of that current of fresh ideas which Matthew Arnold desired, but a measure of indifference which is more stifling than opposition. In any event, Gordon was in no position to take advantage of the intellectual life of the country. His first twelve years in Australia were spent in rural districts, largely alone. The one educated friend he made, Father Woods, was more of a naturalist than a theologian. The books he read were those which happened to come his way, and the *Odes* of Horace could hardly be expected to put him *au courant* with the problems of the times.

II *Ethics and Values*

The basic intellectual problems of the Victorian Age may be divided into two chief categories: on the one hand those of ethics and values, and on the other those of theology and cosmology. We shall take them in that order.

The dominant religious climate in the English-speaking world in the second quarter of the century was Victorian Evangelicalism. Its ethics were based on supernatural sanctions, and its values were supposed to be supernatural values. In practice, the supernatural was mixed with the natural, as was to be expected. Murder is a breach of the Sixth Commandment, but it is also a violation of what civilized men regard as "natural law." Even the Victorian sabbatarianism was a similiar mixture; though based squarely on the Fourth Commandment and observed with Hebraic rigor, it could be defended as a hygienic measure of rest and change. A sermon on the practical disadvantages of drunkenness would begin with an appeal to Biblical authority which declared that "wine is a mocker, strong drink is raging; and whosoever is deceived thereby is not wise" (Proverbs 20, 1).

But the Victorian Age saw the beginning, and more than the beginning, of a shift from a supernatural to a secularist interpretation of life. Benthamite utilitarianism was popularized by John Stuart Mill. Ethical sanctions were increasingly sought, not in divine commands nor in divine prohibitions, but in the consideration of what would promote the greatest happiness for the greatest number.

Victorian Evangelicalism itself was compromised with secular mammonism, partly as a result of the Judaistic strain in Protestantism. Early Judaism regarded worldly prosperity as the proper

reward bestowed by God on the righteous, as the early Psalms
and the Book of Job make clear. It was thus easy for the Victorian Evangelical to interpret prosperity, especially his own, as a
mark of divine approval, as Bulstrode does in *Middlemarch*.
Besides, it was visibly true that those who practiced the Puritan
virtues of thrift, sobriety, and industry did usually, during the
development of the Industrial Revolution, get rich. The idea is
made explicit in Tennyson's *Northern Farmer: New Style*. Moral
worth was identified with respectability, and respectability took
money.

From the middle of the century Christian ethics and humane
values generally were under threat of attack. Philosophic materialism, as distinct from hedonistic materialism, regarded mind
as a function of matter, and was as far from post-Kantian idealism as it was from Biblical Christianity. The crisis sharpened in
1859 with the appearance of *The Origin of Species*. Ethically,
Darwinism was much less important for the logical deductions
which might be drawn from it, or for its apparent contradiction
of Genesis, than for the atmosphere which it created. For man
as a defaced but redeemable image of God was substituted the
concept of man as an improved ape. Moral values became confused with "survival values," and though evolutionary vistas
might stimulate images of a superman there was an uneasy uncertainty as to whether the superman would be an Einstein, a
Stalin, or a Charles Atlas.

To this situation there are several possible responses. One is
the intransigeant resistance to new ideas; this was the response of
Bishop Wilberforce in the 1860's and of William Jennings Bryan
in the 1920's. A second is the attempt to assimilate the new
knowledge to the accepted values—in this instance, Christian
values. Tennyson was at work on this task as he wrote *In Memoriam*. So was Matthew Arnold when he wrote *Literature and
Dogma*, although in his poetry he took a different direction. A
third course is a retreat to hedonism, whether philosophic, as in
Fitzgerald's *Rubaiyat of Omar Khayyam*, or aesthetic, as in
Walter Pater and Oscar Wilde. A fourth is the simple acceptance
of a tragic view of life, such as is implicit in George Eliot and
Thomas Hardy. This response is associated with a high ethical
idealism, basically stoic but with strong Christian overtones of
human sympathy. A fifth possibility is the development of an op-
timistic feeling for the earth, a diluted form of the Romantic na-
turism that we find in Wordsworth. In Canada this appeared
prominently in the poetry of Bliss Carman; in England it is associated with the more positive side of George Meredith.

For Adam Lindsay Gordon, the choice was narrow. He could not take any Christian stance. A man is a Christian for one or more of three reasons: he may have an intuitive awareness of a reality beyond nature, and, specifically, of a Christian "shape" to things; or he may be rationally persuaded by a Christian apologetic; or he may remain within a tradition to which he belongs or to which he chooses to attach himself. None of these affected Gordon. He did not have mystical experiences, Christian or other. He had no philosophic bent, and he was by temperament an anti-traditionalist. But he could not be a hedonist either. Wine, women, and song—or, in more appropriate terms, beer, gins, and ballads—simply did not appeal to him very much. He drank little. His relations with women were as a general rule almost painfully correct. As for song, if we judge by the descriptions of his oral reading,[2] we may suppose that he had not much of an ear for music. Stronger reasons yet kept him from turning to the nature-description of the Canadian poets, or the nature-philosophy found in Bliss Carman and in a good deal of the American poetry of the century. Carman was an educated man, with advanced training in philosophy. Though his "unitrinianism" is desperately naïve, it is rooted in early habits of thought and of discussion with educated men. Besides, the landscape from which Carman drew his inspiration was more friendly to the eye than that in which Gordon spent his adult years. Its trees were greener, its flowers less exotic, and its whole aspect less somber and more human than that of southern Australia.

There remained to Gordon just one basic response to life, and especially to life as it was conceived in the Victorian age, and that was the acceptance of a tragic view of things. Nevertheless, to call it a tragic view and leave it at that would be to oversimplify and to miss the point. If it was tragic, it was tragic with a difference. We need another term for it. Since there is a mode of art which we call "tragi-comedy," we may recognize another which we can call "tragi-melodrama." This is what we find in Gordon.

A speech by the "Chorus" in Anouilh's *Antigone* reminds us of the real difference between tragedy and melodrama. The commonplace idea of melodrama is that of an action in which peril and frustration are first made to seem insurmountable, and then are surmounted or escaped so that the principal characters arrive at a happy ending. Considered more philosophically, the essence of melodrama is not necessarily in the happy ending. What distinguishes melodrama from tragedy is the absence of the sense of *inevitable* catastrophe. For tragedy, the inevitability must lie deep in the characters of the participants and in the nature of the action. It may not be fortuitous, nor dependent merely on external circumstances. The inevitability must be felt, aesthetically perceived, not merely factual. If Goliath had killed David, that would have seemed inevitable to the bystanders, and yet the story would have been melodramatic rather than tragic. A further element is the atmosphere of bravura, the *panache,* which belongs to melodrama. *Cyrano de Bergerac* is pre-eminently melodramatic, not tragic, even though the hero dies by malice with his love unfulfilled. *Oedipus Rex* is a tragedy because Oedipus is driven to his doom by an irresistible destiny working in part through his own character. Adam Lindsay Gordon, in the events of his life, seems a tragic figure, fated like Oedipus; in his thoughts and in his poetry he was nearer to Cyrano.

The values that are woven into his poetry are those of a secular moralism, qualified by those of a Christian civilization. These values are most conveniently considered in the light of the traditional cardinal virtues of fortitude, temperance, prudence, and justice.

The outstanding moral value in Gordon's poetry, as it was the leading trait in his character, is that of fortitude, or courage. It comes into the poetry in two ways. First, it is a value in the narrative poems, and in this respect he is in a long and honorable tradition. Courage is the primary virtue of the epic, from Homer through Beowulf to *The Ring and the Book.* Secondly, it is directly expressed in many of those poems that we would call reflective.

Among the relevant narrative poems one might select, almost at random, "A Legend of Madrid." Although the psychological interest is in the two ladies, the visual center of interest is the matador. The appeal of the bull ring is in its display of courage, plus skill, plus ceremonial pageantry. But courage is the principal thing. The spectacle of mortal danger willfully risked is what provides the fundamental interest. It is an extension, an intensification, of Gordon's sentiment that

> No game was ever worth a rap
>   For a rational man to play,
> Into which no accident, no mishap,
>   Could possibly find its way.
>   ("Ye Wearie Wayfarer," Fytte IV)

There is both courage and glamor in bull-fighting; there is no doubt which of the two appealed most to Gordon.

More striking is the theme in "Ten Paces Off," one of the "Fragmentary Scenes" from "The Road to Avernus." As the title suggests, the scene is that of a duel with pistols. Laurence is the "hero" of the scene, and Forrest is a friend, and apparently his second, who is to give the signal for firing, by dropping a handkerchief. Forrest has a scheme to ensure Laurence's victory. As he drops the handkerchief he will cough; that means that while Laurence's opponent has to watch the handkerchief before taking his final aim, Laurence can keep his eyes on his target, listen for the cough, and get his shot in first. But Laurence does not—cannot—make use of his advantage.

> Though God will never forgive me,
>   Though men make light of my name,
> Though my sin and my shame outlive me,
>   I shall not outlast my shame.

So, when the signal is given he fires in the air and is himself shot through the heart. This is courage displayed on a point of honor, and a typically Gordonian touch.

The poem "Wolf and Hound" shows something of the same but in a different fashion and with a different ending. The narrator is neither a matador nor a cavalier. He is simply a policeman doing his job and feeling rather a fool because he has lost track of his man. He is tired, hungry, baffled, and all but lost. It is by accident that he again comes up with the criminal. He enters the cave where he believes there is an armed and desperate man. He has every disadvantage of position and of light. (One is reminded of the British and German squadrons at the Battle of Cape Coronel in 1914.) But he goes in, and by blind luck survives. There are no heroics. The final line, "I had shot him dead in his den!" suggests nothing more than the completion of an unavoidable but rather dirty and distasteful piece of work. But it meant courage, if not foolhardiness beyond the call of duty. One even wonders if the official police manual would have recommended the procedure.

There is one theme, though, more significant than any of these. Professor H. Northrop Frye has called it the "Thermopylae theme," and has complained of the Canadian poets' failure to make proper use of it.[3] It is the story of men, or women, fighting against heavy odds, outnumbered or outmanoeuvred. It is the theme of the finest battle-piece in Old English poetry:

Hige sceal þe heardra, heorte þe cenre,
mod sceal þe mare, þe ure maegen lytlað
("The Battle of Maldon," ll. 312-13)

Canadian poets had two such stories ready to their hand, in the
fight of Daulac at the Long Sault in 1660, and in the story of
Madeleine de Vercheres' defense of her father's seigneury. The
poets made no effective use of this material.

Gordon in Australia had no such material presented to him.
The Eureka Stockade would not quite serve. So, he reached into
the past and into his imagination for it. *The Feud* takes us back
to the world of the Old Ballads for the scene of the single swords-
man, outnumbered nine to one, but refusing to yield or to fly,
accepting the odds and very nearly winning before being killed
by a blow from the wounded man behind him. Again, at the
close of *Ashtaroth*, he creates a more elaborate narrative with
the same theme. The convent is to be defended against hopeless
odds. The men who survive the first skirmish are convinced that
they are sure to be killed in the next attack, but they have no
thought of surrender or even of regret: "Bring a flask of your
wine, dame, for Eustace and I, / Let us gaily give battle, and
merrily die." The grammar is faulty but the courage is unwaver-
ing. This time it is rewarded; help comes, and although Hugo is
dead the convent is saved.

Courage in the face of death takes two forms, as there are two
forms of the fear of death. There is the fear of death by violence,
which is largely the fear of pain. There is also the fear of death
simply as death, as the final end of earthly experience, and this
also takes various forms. Where it is acute, it is the fear of what
may come after death in the "undiscovered country from whose
bourn / No traveller returns." The Greeks feared boredom; the
medieval Christian feared purgatory; Dr. Johnson feared hell.
Among modern Australians, at least if we judge by the literature,
these fears are vague at best, and not very powerful. There is
another kind of fear which the thought of death brings. It is what
Keats expresses in the sonnet, "When I have fears that I may
cease to be." We fear the sense of incompleteness, of the past
waste of opportunity, of a life which ought to have been different
and which can no longer be made different.

It is the courage corresponding to this last fear, a quiet, country kind of courage that Gordon portrays in the closing stanzas
of "The Sick Stockrider." The stockrider does not fear the loss
of those pleasures that have lightened his life, and what is more
he does not fear, as many of us feel we might, the spectacle of
his own past.

For good undone and gifts misspent and resolutions vain,
   'Tis somewhat late to trouble—This I know,
I should live the same life over, if I had to live again;
   And the chances are I go where most men go.

This kind of fortitude is unspectacular, but admirable in its own way.

We have been dealing with examples of Gordon's presentation of courage through narrative. There is also the direct presentation, in the non-narrative verse, to be considered.

For Gordon's "philosophy" one thinks first of going to "Ye Wearie Wayfarer," and especially to Fytte VIII, subtitled "Finis Exoptatus [A Metaphysical Song]," where we find the best-known, oftenest-quoted lines:

> Life is mostly froth and bubble,
>   Two things stand like stone—
> KINDNESS in another's trouble,
>   COURAGE in your own.

On the surface these are Christian and civilized values, characteristic of much Victorian thought, or pseudo-thought. Dickens, George Eliot, or Mrs. Humphrey Ward might have felt at home with them. But Mrs. Ward's more famous uncle would not have entirely approved. His critical mind, aiming to see things as in themselves they really were, would have led him to ask questions: How does one implement one's kindness? How does one decide which course of action is really the way of courage? A virtue is only a word until it is incarnated in action. The critical mind sees the importance of the words that precede action and determine the main direction that the action will take.

Gordon's words about action, and about courage, are wise as far as they go, and they have probably had their influence in many lives. He also set down some sensible, proverb-like counsels for conduct. But he lacked the critical sense for thought that governs action.

If he made too little of the words that precede action, he made a good deal of the acts that precede action. He sets out a doctrine of play that was enunciated more formally years later in an essay on "The Play of Animals" by Professor J. Arthur Thomson,[4] who described play as "a sham fight before the real battle." For Gordon this the main purpose of play, as he suggests in Fytte IV of "Ye Wearie Wayfarer":

> That brothers and sons might learn
> How a man should uphold the sports of his land,
> And strike his best with a strong right hand,
> And take his strokes in return.

It is also implicit in the lines already cited from the same Fytte, beginning "No game was ever yet worth a rap." In Fytte VII we find a narrower, and exaggerated, statement of the importance of one form of sport:

> Yet if once we efface the joys of the chase
> From the land, and outroot the Stud,
> GOOD-BYE TO THE ANGLO-SAXON RACE!
> FAREWELL TO THE NORMAN BLOOD!

Sport was primarily a training in fortitude, and fortitude was the prime virtue.

The idea is well distributed through the poetry, in statement or commentary. In "Gone," a poem about Burke, the explorer, he writes:

> And well for him, when the timbers start,
> And the stout ship reels and settles below,
> Who goes to his doom with as bold a heart
> As that dead man gone where we all must go.

In "Sunlight on the Sea" he brings in an image of Leonidas and his soldiers feasting before the battle of Thermopylae, and comments, "There's something good in the Spartan creed—," which seems a deliberate understatement.

What does not appear is that hard worship of courage which leads to an intolerant contempt of the less bold. There is a breadth of sympathy in the closing stanza of "A Dedication" to *Bush Ballads and Galloping Rhymes:*

> It matters but little in the long run,
> The weak have some right,
> Some share, in the race that the strong run,
> The fight the strong fight.

He had his own sense of values, within his limitations; he did not waste much energy on those whose sense of values was different from his. He could even show some sympathy with those **who** undervalued his beloved hippolatry:

> We have no wish to exaggerate
> The worth of the sports we prize.
> . . . .
> Good sooth, 'twere a sorry world, I ween,
> If we all went galloping mad.

The remaining cardinal virtues can be dealt with more sum-marily. There is an obvious link between fortitude and temper-ance. Although the first is a virtue of the spirit, or will, and the second is a virtue of the body, we ordinarily tend to think of courage as a physical matter quite as much as temperance. The word "temperance" has indeed many meanings. The fundamental one for our purpose is that of proper restraint, especially the re-straint of bodily passions and desires. The temperate man is the one who, in T. H. Huxley's phrase, has trained his passions to "come to heel." Considered more philosophically, temperance implies a balance of all the human faculties, with nothing in ex-cess and nothing deficient. In poetry, temperance is almost neces-sarily presented by contraries; that is to say, the poet gives us images of the failure of temperance. In Browning's "My last Duchess" we see an excess of pride, an excess (perhaps, on the Duchess' side) of amiability, and a deficiency of human sym-pathy. William Morris' "The Haystack in the Floods" is an inci-dent motivated by murderous lust. Browning's Guido Frances-chini is driven by avarice, pride, and a jealous resentment, all in excess.

There is a good deal of this in Gordon's poetry, though it is not conspicuous. "The Rhyme of Joyous Garde" is the meditation of a man in a state of remorse for the illicit love which had dark-ened his own life and the lives of others. We feel in this poem not the fact of intemperance, or imbalance, that has spoiled Lancelot's life, but only its effects in his state of mind near the close of his life. We are nearer to a truly intemperate life in *Ashtaroth*. Hugo, the Norman baron, has lost the balance of his faculties. In his obsession with knowledge—of an occult sort, we infer—he has neglected other aspects of life. His intemperance consists, not in the excess, but in the deficiency of bodily plea-sure. In *The Feud* we see the excess of avarice and resentment on one side, and that of reckless determination on the other.

The third virtue is prudence. It would seem that prudence (that is, wisdom) is not likely to appear prominently in the struc-ture of Gordon's thought, in spite of the fact that a man may admire most the qualities in which he himself is lacking. We would search in vain for such archetypes of wisdom as Browning's Pope or Tennyson's King Arthur. Still less would we expect the intellectual subtleties of a Bishop Blougram. The Baron Hugo, in *Ashtaroth*, is represented as searching for wisdom, of a sort, but it is a false wisdom that he seeks, and his search, though earnest, is as hollow as Casaubon's scholarship in *Middlemarch*.

There is, however, a less exalted form of prudence for which Gordon's poetry may be called famous. It would be misleading to call it "worldly wisdom," but it consists in wisdom that is useful in the conduct of ordinary life. There are passages that have the pith and practicality of popular proverbs. Some are mere exhortations to an active life, proclaimed as the wisest course.

> Take care of yourself, dull, boorish elf,
>   Though prudent and safe you seem,
> Your pitcher will break on the musty shelf,
>   And mine by the dazzling stream.
>   ("Ye Wearie Wayfarer," Fytte VI)

To wear out and not to rust out is the path of wisdom. Caution, inactivity, and the refusal of risk are not merely unglamorous but foolish.

The most famous of all such passages is in Fytte IV:

> Wear woolen socks, they're the best you'll find;
>   Beware how you leave off flannel;
> And, whatever you do, *don't change your mind*
>   *When once you have picked your panel.*
>   (emphasis added)

In much the same vein, and in the same Fytte, we read:

> Look before you leap, if you like, but if
>   You mean leaping, don't look long.
> . . . .
> Mere pluck, though not in the least sublime,
>   Is wiser than blank dismay.

The whole passage is an exposition of two sides of wordly wisdom. The passages quoted favor boldness. Others give us complementary counsels of caution, as:

> With a bank of cloud in the south south-east,
>   Stand ready to shorten sail;
> Fight shy of a corporation feast;
>   Don't trust to a martingale.

It is significant that the bold lines have been better remembered and oftener quoted than the cautionary.

The specialized wisdom which the word "prudence" generally connotes is not to be found in Gordon. He had no schemes for getting on in life. He did not care to win friends or influence people—except, perhaps, to the reading and appreciation of his poems. The kind of prudence that makes men rich and safe, economically and socially, was not for him. It belonged neither to his life nor to his imagination.

Even the high-hearted wisdom of "The Wearie Wayfarer" does not recur, because in the depths of his mind he knew that it did not really matter much one way or the other, and this feeling increased through the later years of his life. It is all very well to live wisely, but after all,

> Real life is a race through sore trouble,
>   That gains not an inch on the goal,
> And bliss an intangible bubble
>   That cheats an unsatisfied soul.
>   ("Road to Avernus," Scene I)

Life being so, wisdom itself is of limited value. Centuries ago the Preacher said: "For there is no remembrance of the wise more than of the fool for ever; . . . And how dieth the wise man? as the fool." It is all one in the end.

Justice is still less likely than prudence to appear in Gordon's poetry. Justice is the social virtue, and Gordon was by nature a lonely man. There is a notion of justice that came into the Victorian world, and later in a cruder fashion into Australian poetry, but which does not appear in Gordon. The earlier popularity of laissez-faire economics had driven out of men's minds the older concept of the "just price," and had led to the acceptance of ruthless economic struggle as the law of life. Carlyle and Ruskin tried to restore a more humane view. Tennyson, Thomas Hood, and Mrs. Browning, in their different ways, roused emotions sympathetic to the underdog and hostile to the wealthy exploiters. Dickens did the same, more aggressively, on a larger scale, and to a wider audience. Later, in Australia, Henry Lawson was to write of "Faces in the Street." But the ideal of social justice, as we call it nowadays, hardly touched Gordon. He had accepted a lowly position for himself, and the characters he created are generally satisfied with the state of life into which it has pleased God, or fate, to call them. Neither the plight of the poor nor the accidental advantages of the rich move him greatly. He ignores

that side of life. Whether poor or wealthy, and although he spent
by choice most of his life among the lowly, he never quite lost
the instinct of the aristocrat. In his poetry the nobleman has his
code and the stockrider has his, and he has too much respect
for both to wish to bring down the one or to raise the other.

III   *Theology and Cosmology*

As we have seen, Gordon's values were primarily his own, re-
flecting but distantly those of the Victorian period in England.
Behind the values lie basic assumptions of theology and philosophy. In these matters the age was developing a fundamental
split. There was theism, and there was agnosticism, the one beginning to decline and the other rising. Gordon was essentially on
the side of the agnostic, though his poetry is ambivalent. He was
not a man rejecting the notion of God, in the fashion of Bradlaugh
or Ingersoll. Nor was he a man of scientific temper who thought
that all the important problems of life could be solved without
recourse to the hypothesis of God. He was simply caught, like
Matthew Arnold, in "all the doubt and bewilderment of an age
of transition."[5]
Gordon had neither the taste, training, nor talent for serious
philosophical speculation. He had not the university training of
Tennyson and Arnold, nor the omnivorous reading of Browning.
Above all, he did not have the right kind of imagination. His
sense of the numinous was undeveloped or atrophied. He pon-
dered, no doubt, on the nature of life and of humanity and of
"Fate, free will, foreknowledge absolute," but without fruitful result. He read Browning, but it was the Browning of "How They
Brought the Good News from Ghent to Aix" and of "Childe Roland to the Dark Tower Came" that appealed to him; the Browning of the second part of "Saul," or of "A Death in the Desert,"
or of "Christmas Eve" was beyond him. One wonders what, if
he had lived, he would have made of *Ferishtah's Fancies.*
The question is: what, if anything, does Gordon as poet have
to say about the perennial questions? What is the nature of
reality, if any, that he recognizes, and that he, as poet, tries to
construct?
To begin at the center of things, the question of death is ab-
solutely universal, an experience that no one can have the least
hope of escaping. It is dramatic, in contemplation, though not
often in fact. It is final, and yet inconceivable to the average
man in good health. One cannot imagine ceasing to be, nor can

one easily imagine a complete change in the mode of existence. Death is somber at the best, and at most times frightening, not least to the so-called modern man. It is not surprising that a *rationale* of death finds a large place in thought and literature. The Egyptians had a doctrine of an afterlife and a judgment. So had the Muslims centuries later. The Greeks had their images of Hades, a land of disembodied shades and Lethean forgetfulness, from whose endless ennui only the great heroes might hope for deliverance. Early Judaism seems to have had no notion of a life after death except such immortality as a man might achieve through his descendants. Medieval Christianity had an elaborate imagery of hell, purgatory, and heaven, which was in turn taken over and simplified by Protestantism at the Reformation. By the Victorian period the simplification had been exaggerated into vagueness, with childish notions of the dead being turned into angels. This took some of the sting out of death, but only for the simple-minded.

There is another side to this, largely emotional. Death in battle, which we are told was the grand aim in life for the Viking warrior, retained much of its glamor. The death of Nelson is a historical example, and the poetry of Rupert Brooke and Julian Grenfell is a literary expression of the attitude. Between these two, chronologically, lies Robert Louis Stevenson's famous essay, "Aes Triplex," which is an almost lyrical exhortation in prose to indifference toward death and a strenuous use of life.

Gordon's reflective doctrine of death is inevitably difficult to assess. He is not different in this from many, if not most, poets. What would we say of Arnold's view of death if we put together, side by side, "Dover Beach," "Requiescat," and "Rugby Chapel"? What did Shelley really mean by Stanzas 39-55 of *Adonais*?

The second poem in *Sea Spray and Smoke Drift*, entitled "Gone," has the refrain ". . . where we all must go." Gordon seems to have more in mind than the mere blank fact: "Can the spirit feel for the senseless clay / When it once has gone where we all must go?" The lines imply the Victorian, and Greek, assumption. There is a "spirit" that goes—somewhere. The vagueness is a Victorian vagueness. There is neither the Christian hope nor the Greek imagery, but only what we may call in modern times a Cartesian dualism.

The next poem, "Unshriven," concludes with the line "And unshriven to its Maker flies the soul." It is a conventionally Christian image but in its context it tells us little, since the poem is a narrative in an archaic vein, whereas "Gone" has all the marks of a direct expression of Gordon's own feeling.

In the Fourth Fytte of "Ye Wearie Wayfarer" we have the
lines: "It may well be thus where DAVID sings,/ And Uriah joins
in the chorus." The notion of an afterlife persists, though only
as a poetic image, and not by itself to be taken with complete
seriousness. The final stanza of "Bellona" is more cautious:

> Then those who have patiently waited,
> And borne, unresisting, the pain
> Of thy vengeance unglutted, unsated,
> Shall they be rewarded again?
> Then those who, enticed by thy laurels,
> Or urged by thy promptings unblest,
> Have striven and stricken in quarrels,
> Shall they, too, find pardon and rest?
> We know not, yet hope for the best.

This is still no more cautious than Tennyson's

> What hope of answer, or redress?
> Behind the veil, behind the veil.
> (*In Memoriam*, LV)

More forthright is the ending of Gordon's "Ars Longa":

> Life's path is trod at last, and God
> More ready to reprieve is,
> They know, who rest beneath the sod,
> "*Mors gratum, vita brevis.*"

Gordon's best-known passage on this theme is the close of
"The Sick Stockrider":

> Let me slumber in the hollow where the wattle blossoms
>   wave,
>   With never stone or rail to fence my bed;
> Should the sturdy station children pull the bush flowers on
>   my grave,
>   I may chance to hear them romping overhead.

This is a poetic fancy which no one could take seriously, and
yet it will bear some serious thought. There is paradox and contradiction behind it. Neither Christian nor atheist supposes that
the body senses anything from within the grave. Nevertheless
the fancy has a strong hold on our imagination and is not peculiar to the Australian stockrider. Nelson was anxious not to
be buried at sea. The story was told of Abraham Lincoln that

after the death of Ann Rutledge he could hardly bear the thought of snow or rain falling on her grave, as if she could somehow be made uncomfortable by it.[6] It does not matter that the story was not true; the significance is in the fact that it was told and believed. The fancy is reflected in literature, in *Wuthering Heights* by Heathcliff's arrangements for the burial of Cathy and himself, and in Rudyard Kipling's "The Rhyme of the Mary Gloster." The notion dies hard. We keep on feeling that it matters where and how our bodies lie, even though we know that it does not. Seldom has the idea been given a simpler more direct, or more felicitious expression that in these lines of Gordon's.

"The Swimmer" contains a Swinburnean statement opposite to the foregoing:

> Under the sea or the soil (what matter?
> The sea and the soil are under the sun),
> As in the former days in the latter
> The sleeping or waking is known of none,
> Surely the sleeper shall not awaken
> To griefs forgotten or joys forsaken,
> For the price of all things given and taken,
> The sum of all things done and undone.

This is a little ambiguous, but it seems to say that death is the end of all sensation. The three stanzas following give support to the interpretation that death puts a final end to consciousness, and that dead men, as Swinburne held, "rise up never." In comparing this passage with the one quoted just earlier, it must be remembered that "The Sick Stockrider" is a dramatic monologue whereas "The Swimmer" is a lyric which apparently expresses Gordon's own thought.

In "No Name" there is a new direction. At the close of the poem the image is that of a soul which may be punished or rewarded after death.

> And I know that if, here or there, alone,
> I found him, fairly and face to face,
> Having slain his body, I would slay my own,
> That my soul to Satan his soul might chase.
> He hardens his heart in the public way—
> Who am I? I am but a nameless churl;
> But God will put all things straight some day—
> Till then may your sleep be a sound one, girl!

In "De Te" he comes back to the attitude of vague hopefulness characteristic of his age and still found in ours:

> No man may shirk the allotted work,
>   The deed to do, the death to die;
> At least I think so,—neither Turk,
>   Nor Jew, nor infidel am I,—
> And yet I wonder when I try
>   To solve one question, may or must,
> And shall I solve it by and bye,
>   Beyond the dark, beneath the dust?
>   I trust so, and I only trust.

This is Tennyson's "infant crying for the light:/And with no language but a cry."

Lastly, there are two poems which express opposite sides of Gordon's thoughts about death. "Doubtful Dreams," as the title suggests, gives us mere uncertainty: "We know not whether they slumber/Who waken on earth no more," and the ending of "The Rhyme of Joyous Garde" gives us a Christian picture:

> Yet if all things change to the glory of One
> Who for all illdoers gave His Own sweet Son,
>   To His goodness so shall He change ill,
> When the world as a wither'd leaf shall be,
> And the sky like a shrivell'd scroll shall flee,
> And souls shall be summon'd from land and sea,
>   At the blast of His bright archangel.

Again we must remember that "The Rhyme of Joyous Garde" is dramatic, whereas in "Doubtful Dreams" Gordon is speaking, so far as we can judge, *in propria persona.*

The question of death is crucial, especially in view of the rise of philosophic materialism in the nineteenth century. If mind is only a function of matter, as Nietzsche asserted in the nineteenth century and the behaviorist psychologists in the twentieth, then there can be no life after death. If matter is a function of mind, then there may be. On this question, not surprisingly, Gordon wavered. What is surprising is that, on balance, the sense for immortality seems to preponderate. It is a feeling, not a reasoned doctrine nor even a theological postulate. It is a residuum of the assumptions of his childhood training, the Victorian assumption that somehow, in some fashion, there was a life beyond the grave. He did not wholeheartedly believe it, but he could never altogether stop believing it. The state of mind was an epitome of the Victorian age.

Death is only a fact in human experience. The framework of experience itself is the universe in which we live. The poet's universe, which depends to some degree on his theological assumptions, is the most fundamental thing about him. What is the universe really like and what does it really mean? This question is implicit in all serious literature. Because men's intuitions differ, their visions of the nature and meaning of the universe differ. Shelley's is not the same as Dante's nor is Eliot's the same as Shelley's.

The attempt to find a concept of God takes one of four main directions. One is the blank negative of atheism. The second is that of God in the universe and roughly co-terminous with it; in other words, one of the forms of pantheism. The third is that of God as creator and supervisor, separate, or at least separable, from the whole system of nature which we inhabit. The fourth is the epicurean notion of God as separate from, and generally indifferent to, the affairs of men.

When we consider this question in Gordon's poems we must again make the distinction between the two sorts of expression. One is the direct expression, in separate and quotable passages. The other is the tenor of the whole body of poetry, the tone of it, and the deductions one would make from that tonality. We shall begin with something about the separate passages.

Fytte V of "Ye Wearie Wayfarer" ends:

> By the will of a just, yet a merciful Power,
> Less bitter, perchance, in the mystic hour,
> When the wings of the shadowy angel lower,
> Than man in his blindness teaches!

"Laudamus," at the end of *Bush Ballads and Galloping Rhymes*, is well sprinkled with lines like "The Lord shall slay—," and "The Lord!—his mercy—." Between these two there are several references to God, but not many and not usually meaningful. They are often merely conventional ways of expressing feelings. When a man says "Thank God," he is not necessarily committing himself to a theological position; he may be, and usually is, expressing relief in a conventional fashion. When Gordon does seem to mean something by bringing in the idea of God, it is in the spirit of the penultimate line of "No Name," "But God will put all things straight some day—." The ending of "Ars Longa" is in a similar mood. At most, this comes to no more than the Victorian half-belief in an ultimate power, vaguely kind, who will eventually put right the ills of this life.

If we set aside the "proof-texts" to be found in the poems, and think instead of their tone, their atmosphere, our conclusions may be different. The world of Gordon's poetry, taken in a lump, is a hard world, a world of frustration and death, a world in which a man may have a brief period of enjoyment but in which the shadows quickly fall around him. It is reminiscent in many ways of Old English elegiac poetry such as "The Wanderer." God's control of the universe is hardly a live issue. At the best we are ciphers "in God's vast creation" ("Ye Wearie Wayfarer," Fytte VIII).

Returning for a moment to the question of values, we must admit that there are certain appropriate responses to life as Gordon sees it, and one is *carpe diem*—such a response as Arnold pictures in capsule form in "Mycerinus." There is something of this in Gordon. At least there is a trace of the acceptance of mere living such as governs the first half of Browning's "Saul":

> The lungs with the living gas grow light,
>   And the limbs feel the strength of ten,
> While the chest expands with its madd'ning might,
>   GOD'S GLORIOUS OXYGEN.
>   ("Ye Wearie Wayfarer," Fytte VII)

But Gordon wears his *carpe diem* with a difference. The "day" is to be "seized" not simply for enjoyment but for accomplishment. We are to "live and labour / Till yon goal be won" (Fytte VIII). The weakness here is that there is no goal. The labor is itself the goal. The aim of life is to practice kindness and courage along the way, but the way leads nowhere. It is a pilgrim's progress without a Celestial City. Therefore Gordon, and the reader who is in sympathy with him, is thrown back on a stoical view of life which is simply one of tragic endurance. It is easy to undervalue this. Merely to get through life without gross moral failure is no small accomplishment. To go on in the face of difficulty, "Helping every feeble neighbour, / Seeking help from none" is an ideal not to be despised. It was the best that Gordon's premises could lead him to.

Three elements are involved. There is Gordon himself, with his character and his temperament; there is the age in which he lived; and there is the country in which he lived. The second of these is the one we are mainly considering here. The first has been implicit throughout, and the third is reserved for later consideration.

Gordon was a Victorian poet, though a diluted one. He had the religious posture of the Victorian age; that is, a wavering between faith and unfaith, with the balance on the side of unfaith. He was not anti-clerical, nor was he a militant atheist. He seems not to have been quite sure what he was. He did not wrestle with doubts like Robert Elsmere or Ernest Pontifex. He rather took his doubts for granted, and made something out of them. That something was a stoicism (with a small "s") which had a tincture of Christian feeling in it. It was a little like the Old English poems in which we find both Christian and pagan elements mingled but not fused. In chemical terms, it is a colloid, not a solution.

Gordon was not much of a "thinking man," and he was certainly not a philosophical poet. But so far as the thought and the themes of his poetry go, they are Victorian. In their expression they are necessarily Victorian. He lived in, and in his way expressed, some of the Victorian states of mind.

CHAPTER 6

The Emotions

I *The Place and Nature of Emotions*

THUS far we have been considering the stories which Gordon put into verse, and the ideas which can be discovered in it. But the principal ingredient of poetry is generally thought to be emotion. Not only has Wordsworth described poetry as "the spontaneous overflow of powerful feelings," which "takes its origin from emotion recollected in tranquillity," but the late R. G. Collingwood, in *The Principles of Art*, argues that the essence of art is the precise expression of emotion. A. E. Housman, in his lecture on "The Name and Nature of Poetry" actually defines poetry as what causes the kind of physical reaction by which psychologists attempt to define and identify emotion.

It is necessary to distinguish between the direct and the indirect expression of emotion. Many familiar poems are direct expressions. When Wordsworth wrote "I wandered lonely as a cloud," or the "Tintern Abbey Lines" he was expressing his own emotions, the feelings that came to him at a certain time and in certain circumstances. So was Byron when he wrote the "Ocean" passage in *Childe Harold's Pilgrimage* (IV, 179-84), and Keats when he wrote the sonnet "On First Looking into Chapman's Homer." But there is much poetry which is not a direct expression of feeling at all. There is intense feeling in Browning's "Soliloquy of the Spanish Cloister," but it is not Browning's. Whatever of emotion there may be in "The Love Song of J. Alfred Prufrock" need not be attributed to Mr. Eliot; in spite of his bowler hat and rolled umbrella, there were few men of his time to whom the mermaids sang more clearly than to him. There is, therefore, the indirect expression of emotion—emotion through narrative and emotion through dramatic poetry. Eliot himself has given us the phrase for it, the "objective correlative" of the emotion to be expressed.

However expressed, the validity of emotion in art depends on its being in some sense universal. The emotion is one which can be shared, actually or potentially, by the reader. The man who has known the exhilaration of fresh air, solitude, and the color of wild flowers may respond directly to Wordsworth's poem on the daffodils. So may the man who has not known it, but who can sense imaginatively what such an experience would be like. And, to take a very different work, *Hamlet* is among other things an expression of those emotions felt by a man in a dilemma, a situation in which he feels simultaneously that he must act and that he cannot act. Since every civilized man does occasionally find himself in such a situation, *Hamlet* becomes, on these terms, an expression of a universal feeling.

Art is both communication and expression at the same time and in the same act of creation. In other words, the poet is communicating both with his readers and with himself. It is only in the act of shaping his poem that he is enabled fully to realize the precise emotion which he has experienced. The public speaker who was asked before the meeting what his speech would be about, and who replied, "How do I know what it will be about until I hear what I have to say?" was enunciating, though he did not know it, a doctrine of aesthetics.

What emotions have we to express? The psychologists are not altogether in agreement, but they do provide us with a basic scheme. According to Watson, there are three original emotions: fear, rage, and love. Another formula recognizes "four emotional systems of anger, fear, joy and sorrow."[1] From these we can construct a scheme which will be useful for the examination of the poetry. Joy and sorrow are recognizable as two aspects of the emotion of love. There is joy when the loved object, whatever it may be, is present; and sorrow when it is absent, unattainable, or threatened. Contrasted with these are the negative emotions of fear and anger.

By putting up with some artificiality, we can catalogue those objects of love that may find expression in poetry. The usual one, which anyone thinks of first when the world "love" is mentioned, has to do with a specialized affection for a member of the opposite sex. The second commonest use of the term denotes an affection for any other human beings, such as the members of one's own family. The third object of love is the world of external nature. This seems to have begun in the Romantic period, and to have persisted thereafter, most conspicuously in Canadian poetry of the late nineteenth century. The love of pets, whether cats, dogs, or horses, is an amalgam of the second and third of these, but is closest to the second. Fourthly, there is the love of certain abstractions or "ideals"; patriotism, the love of liberty, and religious loyalties are often of this kind. Fifthly, there is a love of God, felt as an actual experience, generally regarded as peculiar to only a few people called, or miscalled, "mystics." Sixth and last is the "love of life." The object of love in this sense might be defined as the totality of human experience, but it usually means the sense-experience, especially of youth.

Each of these forms of love has its corresponding sorrow, well known in poetry. For the first there is unrequited love, or the death of the beloved. For the second, there is, similarly, loss or estrangement. For the third, there is the longing of the city-pent man for the country. The fourth gives us such feelings as Wordsworth puts into the sonnet beginning "It is not to be thought of that the Flood." The fifth, which takes the form of spiritual dryness, is much complained of by the professed religious but seldom finds its way into poetry. The sixth, on the negative side, is that loss of bodily and emotional vigor which is complained of in old age, or the loss of sensitivity in middle age which appears in Coleridge's "Dejection: An Ode."

We now turn to Gordon's poems to see how he dealt with these emotions, which ones he expressed, and how effective was his expression.

II *Love, Joy, and Sorrow*

Romantic love played a relatively small part in the life of Adam Lindsay Gordon. The one powerful attachment of his early days came to nothing. Then he went to Australia, where he flirted occasionally and married once. The flirtations, with one possible exception, were not serious, and the marriage was not passionate. One would expect, therefore, little love-poetry in the ordinary sense. That is, one would expect little of the kind of love-poetry that seems to arise out of the writer's own deeply felt experience, such as Arnold's "Marguerite" poems are generally judged to be. Three poems make up Gordon's whole tale, and one of those is doubtful to the last degree.

The one clear example is in the poem "To My Sister," written just before he sailed from England. Three stanzas, twenty-four lines, are devoted to his lost love. They begin:

> I loved a girl not long ago,
>   And, till my suit was told,
> I thought her breast as fair as snow,
>   'Twas very near as cold;

and they end:

> But absent friends are soon forgot,
>   And in a year or less
> 'Twill doubtless be another's lot
>   Those very lips to press!

Tho whole passage is a straightforward statement of what had happened in his last interview with Jane Bridges, in smooth and competent verse, but it is not highly poetical. The passage includes a declaration that "Those words I never spoke before, / Nor ever shall again." This is the conventional feeling of the newly rebuffed lover, seldom to be taken seriously. Gordon meant them more seriously than most, as it turned out. When he came to marry, years later, he disclaimed all "romantic nonsense."

"Whisperings in Wattle-Boughs," published in *Sea Spray and Smoke Drift,* contains a stanza (the fifth) which looks like an oblique reference to his early love. The second, third, and fourth stanzas are addressed respectively to "father mine," "sister dear," and "ancient friend." The fifth follows:

> Oh, whisper buried love, is there rest and peace above?—
>   There is little hope or comfort here below;—
> On your sweet face lies the mould, and your bed is strait
>   and cold—
>   Near the harbour where the sea-tides ebb and flow.

The image is false to the fact, since Jane Bridges outlived Gordon, but in view of its placing in the pattern of the poem we are led to assume that it is derived from the memory of his early, unlucky love. The important consideration is the change in mood which the change in fact reveals. The cold, rejecting "belle dame sans merci" is replaced by the sympathetic pathos of the dead sweetheart.

The third and dubious instance is "Thora's Song" from *Ashtaroth,* reprinted separately in *Bush Ballads and Galloping Rhymes.* Ostensibly, this has nothing to do with Jane, or with Gordon either. It is dramatic, and entirely within the story. It is the lament of a woman, not of a man. The opening line, "We severed in autumn early" may be mere coincidence; and anyway Gordon's farewell interview with Jane was about the beginning of August, which is hardly in the autumn. Despite all this, we may justly think that the roots of the poem are in the emotions of Gordon's past, with its experience of separation and of coming "not back again."

One other poem has to do with love, directly, but love significantly takes a second place in it. The opening piece of *Sea Spray and Smoke Drift* is "Podas Okus," a monologue spoken by Achilles on his deathbed, to Briseis. The opening is "Am I waking? Was I sleeping? / Dearest, are you watching yet?" But it is quickly clear that Achilles is not thinking much about Briseis, but about his former comrades-in-arms, about his glory, about how "None can baffle Jove's decree," and about the multiform "doom" that brought about and surrounded the Trojan war. The ending of the poem suggests the balance of Achilles' emotions:

> Lightly lay your red lips, kissing,
>   On this cold mouth, while your thumbs
> Lie on these cold eyelids pressing—
>   Pallas! thus thy soldier comes.

At the climax, it is not Briseis that fills Achilles' mind and his emotions, but Pallas and his own soldiership. It hardly needs to be added that this was characteristic of Gordon's own makeup.

Apart from these lyric, or semi-lyric, expressions of romantic love, the theme finds little place in Gordon's verse. What there is, is almost entirely conventional, if not commonplace. Hugo, in *Ashtaroth*, is torn for a time by an illicit passion for Agatha, but that passion (which also comes to nothing) is a minor theme. *The Feud*, earlier, contains love as well as avarice and fighting, but the story is drawn from a well-known source and Gordon adds little to it except for some small expansion of detail. In "The Rhyme of Joyous Garde" the thoughts of the aging Lancelot are as much with Arthur and Arthur's enemies as they are with Guinevere. Moreover, it was not Gordon's love-poetry that his earliest public responded to. It was quite other emotions and other experiences which, wedded to verse probably not quite immortal, won Gordon his unique following among Australian readers, and those overseas.

It is not the joy of love, but the sorrow of love, that Gordon expresses. The joy of love he seems not to have experienced, and he made no attempt to deal with it. He had experienced the loss of

love, though in an adolescent fashion, and that was what he
kept to.

When we come to the second form of love, which might be
called, for short, "fraternal love," the case is different. We would
not expect much love for his family to appear in the poetry. He
left home before he was twenty; he never returned, and, so far
as is now known, was never in effective communication with his
family again. He felt that he had disgraced them, and that they
had fallen short in their sympathy with him. Of these two feelings, the first appears to have been the stronger. Whatever he
may have felt, he did not show resentment, except by one hint,
in "Early Adieux":

> My mother is a stately dame,
>   Who oft would chide with me;
> She saith my riot bringeth shame,
>   And stains my pedigree.

There seems to be a touch of irony in these lines, but nothing
more.

Family feeling does come to light in several places. These
have mainly to do with his father, and reflect darkly happy
memories. The Third Fytte of "Ye Wearie Wayfarer" opens with
a memory of "some words my father said." The clear expression
of this feeling is in the second stanza of "Whisperings in Wattle-
Boughs":

> Oh, tell me, father mine, ere the good ship cross'd the brine,
>   On the gangway one mute hand-grip we exchang'd,
> Do you, past the grave, employ, for your stubborn, reckless
>   boy,
>   Those petitions that in life were ne'er estrang'd?

These lines reveal, at the least, how Gordon came to regard his
father in later years, when time had mellowed his memories. It
is to be noted, too, that in the three poems of exile, "To My
Sister," "An Exile's Farewell," and "Early Adieux" (two of them
certainly and the third presumably early verses written at the
time of his migration), Gordon's father is not mentioned at all—
except as he is included by the word "parents." Interpretation
here is altogether conjectural, but the soundest guess would seem
to be that Gordon's memory of his father was, at this time, sharp
and painful. His mother had disapproved of him, but he had not
minded that much. She had shut herself out of his world, and if

she was grieved by his behavior, that was her problem. But he did feel differently about his father, and the sense of having let his father down was one which he could not then bear to think about. It was only years later that he was able to let his feeling for his father come to light, and find an expression in his poetry.

It was neither his family nor his sweetheart(s) that aroused the expressions of human love to be found in his best-remembered poetry. It was the friend and the co-worker for whom these expressions were reserved. The most significant document here is not "The Sick Stockrider," but "The Rhyme of Joyous Garde." The story behind the poem is the familiar Arthurian legend of illicit passion, which brought to an end the fair, best hope of the Arthurian kingdom. In *The Idylls of the King*, this is where Tennyson places the emphasis. The affair, the scandal, is a slow staining spreading outward, creating cynicism, puzzlement, and finally indifference and contempt toward knightly vows. William Morris puts the emphasis on love, interpreted as real love between Lancelot and Guinevere—a love tragically rendered illegitimate by the accident of a loveless marriage. Gordon's emphasis is different from either.

"The Rhyme of Joyous Garde" begins with two stanzas of descriptive introduction. Then, following a transitional stanza beginning "For the days recall what the nights efface," the fourth stanza reads:

> Would God I had died the death that day
> When the bishop blessed us before the fray
>   At the shrine of the Saviour's Mother;
> We buckled the spur, we braced the belt,
> Arthur and I—together we knelt,
> And the grasp of his kingly hand I felt
>   As the grasp of an only brother.

This is the governing mood of the poem. The sense of guilt is strong, and is emphasized by the climax of the last six stanzas. But the main tenor of the poem is not that of sin against God or of sin against society, but of the sin against Arthur. It is a sin against friendship. He had loved Arthur, and he had betrayed him. This is established in the fourth stanza. It does not need to be reiterated, and it is not. A few touches, scattered through the poem, give it all the emphasis it needs. Two lines in the twenty-sixth stanza will serve as an example: "And the once loved knight, was he there to save / That knightly king who that knighthood gave?" The point of these lines, when they are read

88

in the context of the whole poem, is not the hierarchical relationship of king to knight, but the relationship of knight to knight,
one of them being the king.

The emotion of the poem is a sorrowful one, of love betrayed.
But the love is not that of man and woman; it is the love of man
and man. It is the love of two men engaged together in a common life, with common aims, who had shared experiences of life-
and-death struggles. And this emotion is achieved without under-
valuing the other. The passion of Lancelot's love for Guinevere
is included.

> When I well-nigh swoon'd in the deep drawn bliss,
> Of that first long, sweet, slow, stolen kiss,
> I would gladly have given for less than this
> Myself, with my soul's salvation.

What is more, the erotic love is not pictured as mere physical
passion.

> I would languish thus in some loathsome den,
> As a thing of naught in the eyes of men,
> In the mouths of men as a by-word,
> Through years of pain, and when God saw fit,
> Singing His praises my soul should flit
> To the darkest depth of the nethermost pit,
> If *hers* could be wafted skyward.
>
>   (Stanza 34)

The love for Guinevere was real love, the love which seeks the
welfare of the beloved at any cost. But in the full context of the
poem, Lancelot's love for Guinevere seems an incident—not a
trivial incident (quite the contrary) but essentially an incident
nonetheless. It is the relationship between Lancelot and Arthur
that strikes home to us.

"The Sick Stockrider" shows one similarity to "The Rhyme of
Joyous Garde." The same emotion of friendship is established at
the opening of the poem, and is maintained only by oblique hints
through the rest of it. The apostrophe of the first four lines,

> Hold hard, Ned! Lift me down once more, and lay me in
>   the shade.
>   Old man, you've had your work cut out to guide
> Both horses, and to hold me in the saddle when I sway'd,
>   All through the hot, slow, sleepy, silent ride.

sets an emotional pattern. It is made implicitly clear at the beginning, and it becomes explicit a little later in the poem, that "Ned" is no chance Good Samaritan. He has had a close, long-standing relationship with the speaker. In fact, this is "mate-ship," but that is another matter. Ned and the speaker have, like Arthur and Lancelot, been through much together. The "we" that appears and reappears ("We led the hunt throughout, Ned," for example) tells us that, and suggests even more than it tells. Ned has been engaged in an office of friendship, trying to get his sick friend home. At least, we suppose he is trying to get him home; the destination of the ride is artistically left to the imagination, but the lines "Five miles we used to call it from our homestead to the place / Where the big tree spans the roadway like an arch;" give us a sufficient hint.

There are two opposed but complementary emotions in the poem. One is the remembered joy of old accomplishment and old friendship. All this belongs to the past, but it is heart-lifting to remember. The emotion of sorrow, it is important to note, also belongs to the past. The stockrider is not feeling sorry for himself, except in the fact that almost all his old friends are gone. It is the death of other men, not his own, that affects him. The two feelings, of joy and of sorrow, come together in the lines:

> In these hours when life is ebbing, how those days when
>   life was young
>   Come back to us; how clearly I recall
> Even the yarns Jack Hall invented, and the songs Jem
>   Roper sung;
>   And where are now Jem Roper and Jack Hall?

When the poem is seen in this light, the final sixteen lines appear as a coda. The four lines beginning "I've had my share of pastime, and I've done my share of toil" make a transition, and a skillful transition. Then follows the conclusion, with its acceptance of both life and death, ending in the funerary instructions and the memorable image of the grave.[2]

Another poem with the double image of the joys and the sorrows of friendship, and with the sorrow more than ever predominating, is "Sunlight on the Sea," subtitled "The Philosophy of a Feast." It begins in a joyful mood: "Make merry, comrades, eat and drink / (The sunlight flickers on the sea)." The end of the first stanza sums up the positive aspect of the scene.

> I see you feasting round me still,
>   All gay of heart and strong of limb;
> Make merry, friends, your glasses fill,
>   The lights are growing dim.

The very next line brings in the mournful side, with "I miss the voice of one I've heard." From here on there is maintained the contrast between the pleasure of the feast, and the thought of those who are absent or dead. The whole poem is a polarity of joy and sorrow, but the joy is slightly artificial. The reality of fellowship is in its loss, and the final line of each stanza is "The lights are growing dim." This line is a refrain, and its sense changes as the poem goes on. At the end of the first stanza it seems to mean: the toil and danger of the day are now over and as the light wanes we can relax and enjoy our ease. In the intervening stanzas it takes an increasingly darker meaning. The dimming lights are a symbol of death, and of the number of the dead (or absent) which increases as time goes on. At the close, it has a cosmic significance. Death closes all, for every man and even, perhaps, for the world itself.

The important feature of "Sunlight on the Sea" is the essential nobility of the poem. What it says is not "eat, drink, and be merry, for tomorrow we die," but rather "eat, drink, and be merry, although tomorrow we may die." It is the spirit of Stevenson's *Aes Triplex*, though in a more limited form. This is underlined by the sixth stanza, with its image of the Spartan soldiers feasting undismayed before Thermopylae.

An entirely different poem is the one called "Laudamus," the final piece in *Bush Ballads and Galloping Rhymes* as it first appeared. This is a poem of hate, rather than of love, although it is hate that is ending and in the process of turning into reconciliation. Two men have loved one woman. The speaker addresses his rival as "Brother," which may mean one of two things. Either the rivals were brothers by blood, or they were former friends whose friendship was broken and turned to hatred by their rivalry for the woman. In any case, the woman has died, the reason for their hatred is gone. The sense of the title is clarified in the fourth stanza:

> Let us thank the Lord for His bounties all,
>   For the brave old days of pleasure and pain,
> When the world for both of us seem'd too small—
>   Though the love was void and the hate was vain—

The "pleasure and pain" duality is made explicit, and here for once the joy, at least potentially, over-crowds the sorrow. The reconciliation which the poem implies is felt as permanent. It will go even beyond the grave. The poem ends:

> We shall meet, my friends, in the spirit land—
> Will our strife renew? Nay, I dare not trust,
>   For the grim, great gulf that cannot be spann'd
> Will divide us from her. The Lord is just,
>   She shall not be thrust where our spirits stand.

For the most part, though, Gordon accepts the proposition that love of our fellowmen (as distinguished from love of our fellowman) entails more of sadness than of joy. The joy is temporary and the sorrow is inevitable. Friendships, no matter how warm, are made to be broken, either by betrayal as in "The Rhyme of Joyous Garde" or by death as in "The Sick Stockrider." And yet, Gordon succeeds very nearly in keeping a balance between the two emotions of joy and sorrow. The love and fellowship of man with other men is not only a real joy while it lasts, but when it has ended it does not cease to exist. The past, because it is the past, is unchangeable. It is real and it remains. This is the point, or one of the points, of the sick stockrider's reminiscences. The joys of the past adventures which the two men have shared are a part of the pattern of their lives, which is permanent. Death completes the pattern, and by adding to it alters it, but it does not destroy the good things that have already been woven into it.

The third species of love is the love of external nature, of landscape and of trees and flowers. It is peculiarly prominent in the poetry of the "colonies" during the nineteenth century, and especially so in Canada, where is produced the "Maple Leaf School" in the 1880's and 1890's. Gordon's treatment, or lack of treatment, of nature is one of the counts made against him in the indictment for not being sufficiently "Australian." He aroused indignation by writing in "A Dedication" to *Bush Ballads and Galloping Rhymes* of "lands where bright blossoms are scentless, / And songless bright birds." Yet one supposes that the lines are literally true. The writer cannot answer for the bright flowers, being somewhat deficient in the sense of smell. Nor has he any skill as a bird-watcher, or bird-listener. But he does feel sure that the kookaburra (though perhaps not bright enough to qualify as evidence) has not much of a song. The fact remains, nevertheless, that there has existed a feeling that Gordon did not do right by the landscape of his adopted country.

There are several reasons for this. The first is that Gordon was
not a landscape poet, in any sense. He was a poet of human
activity and human thoughts and feelings. The landscape was
never anything but setting and background, where needed, to a
scene or story of activity. Such primarily descriptive passages as
Harpur or Kendall wrote (or, in Canada, Lampman or Roberts
or Campbell) were simply not among his interests. Secondly,
much of his material was drawn unashamedly from England and
from the past. Even "How We Beat the Favourite," one of his
most popular poems among Australians, is set in the English Cots-
wolds. And the stories that he drew from a distant past, such as
"The Romance of Britomarte," necessitated a setting far from
Australia. Australia, in that sense, had no past. Thirdly, he was
extremely nearsighted, and could not possibly be aware of the
landscape except in a general, and blurred, fashion. Last, and
least, it is true that to some extent landscape is landscape all over
the world. It is a matter of experience that the Canadian who
travels to England will see many scenes which, although they
have the flavor of England, remind him also of some stretch of
country which he has seen in his own homeland. We can demonstrate this fact in Gordon's verse. Take these lines from "Visions
in the Smoke," the First Part of "Hippodramia; or, Whiffs from
the Pipe."

> Rest, and be thankful! On the verge
>   Of the tall cliff, rugged and grey,
> At whose granite base the breakers surge,
>   And shiver their frothy spray. . . .
> . . . .
> There'll be storm, and rattle, and tempest soon,
>   When the heavens are overcast.
> The neutral tint of the sullen sea
>   Is flecked with the snowy foam,
> And the distant gale sighs drearilie,
>   As the wanderer sighs for his home.

We may suppose this descriptive material to be authentic enough,
although we may have reservations about the word "granite." It
is doubtful if Gordon could have distinguished granite from
sandstone at any distance. But it is not particularly characteristic
of Australia. There are cliffs and breakers, and spray, and foam,
and gales on the coasts of Scotland, or Nova Scotia, or British
Columbia, or Hong Kong.

It is true that in Gordon's poetry there are no wallabies and not much wattle. We are not bombarded with dingoes, wombats, saltbush, malee scrub, nor even gum-trees. If he regarded the kangaroo as the "spirit of Australia" he gives no sign of it. This does not matter much. These are details such as any tourist might put into a travelogue.

No; the real charge against Gordon in this regard is that he does not render the tone, the "feel," of the Australian landscape. That tone is fundamentally different from the landscape of England. The color is different. Even Gordon's limited vision might be presumed to be aware of that. The Australian trees, especially when seen in a mass, are nearer to blue-gray than to the bright green of England. And there is the loneliness of the countryside. Even today, the visitor from North America is struck by the comparative isolation of the Australian stations, different from the farm-lined roads of Ontario or New England. To a man coming from England more than a century ago the contrast should have been even more striking. The distances from one center of population to another, and the roughness of the country between, ought to have been noticeable, if not awe-inspiring, to one who had been used to the tidy, cosy humanity of the countryside in the English shires. There is almost no recognition of this in Gordon, except for a touch of it, but an obscure touch, in "The Sick Stockrider."

One further explanation stands out. Of all the various aspects and forms of nature, the one which most attracted Gordon, at least in his maturer years, was the sea—and the sea is pretty much the same everywhere, especially when we remember that he never saw the beaches of New South Wales or Queensland.

But what difference does all this make? The fact is that he took relatively little interest in landscape. It was not his *métier*. And who is to say that it ought to have been? We do not blame a dentist for not removing tonsils, nor a surgeon for not filling teeth.

Though there was little of the Romantic love of natural scenery in Gordon, it was not entirely absent. It was in his life, and in his poetry, though subordinate and subdued. He seems to have had a strong affection for the rural setting of the cottage at Dingley Dell, even though, as it turned out, he did not live there for long. In his poetry, he opens the "Dedication" to *Bush Ballads and Galloping Rhymes* with forty-eight lines of which forty-seven are on this theme.

> Whence gather'd?—The locust's glad chirrup
> May furnish a stave;

> The ring of a rowel and stirrup,
> The wash of a wave,
> The chaunt of the marsh frog in rushes,
> That chimes through the pauses and hushes
> Of nightfall, the torrent that gushes,
> The tempests that rave.

The third line of this stanza is the only break in the catalogue of natural beauty. The culmination is in the sixth stanza, one of the oftenest quoted of his verses.

> In the Spring, when the wattle gold trembles
> 'Twixt shadow and shine,
> When each dew-laden air draught resembles
> A long draught of wine;
> When the sky-line's blue burnish'd resistance
> Makes deeper the dreamiest distance,
> Some song in all hearts hath existence,—
> Such songs have been mine.

The stanza just cited calls for two comments. The first is that in the passage which it concludes Gordon does come unusually close to giving us the feel of the Australian lanscape. Besides the "wattle gold" and the "dreamiest distance," and setting aside the songless birds and the scentless flowers, we have "Insatiable Summer," "sere woodlands," "sad wildernesses," "faint flocks and herds," "dry deserts," and "trunks Eucalyptian." It is a respectable catalogue. The second comment is that if Gordon had ended the poem at the end of the sixth stanza, it would have been misleading. The reader would have been entitled to object, and to retort, "Such songs have *not* been yours." The next poem in the volume was "The Sick Stockrider," in which natural scenery plays a part, but a different part and a subordinate part. Then, following "The Swimmer," which is in part a nature-poem, we have "From the Wreck," which contains but hardly features the landscape, "No Name," "Wolf and Hound," "De Te," and "How We Beat the Favourite," which last is not Australian at all, except in spirit. Of the remaining poems in the book not one has to do with Australian scenery, with the possible and insignificant exception of "A Song of Autumn." Indeed, "Doubtful Dreams" begins "Aye, snows are rife in December, / And sheaves are in August yet." Not in Australia they aren't!

Now a distinction has to be made. Gordon was an outdoor man and his poetry is outdoor poetry. But there is a difference between an outdoor man and an outdoor poet. The outdoor poet, in this sense of the term, loves the countryside in a way which impels him to observe it closely and describe it attentively, often in photographic detail. Gordon, in his poetry at all events, did not love the countryside in that way. He loved *being* in the countryside; he loved the experience of the open air. The difference is subtle but important.

There is one exception. The sea did come to exercise a power over him, which appears in his poetry, especially in "The Song of the Surf." The first two stanzas, beginning:

> White steeds of ocean, that leap with a hollow and
>   wearisome roar
> On the bar of ironstone steep, not a fathom's length
>   from the shore

is true landscape—or, rather, seascape—poetry. The remaining two stanzas introduce the image of a drowned corpse, and a rebuke to foolish mortals:

> Think'st thou the wave that shatters questioneth His
>   decree?
> Little to us it matters, and naught it matters to thee.

"The Swimmer" is in the same category. It begins with three stanzas of descriptive matter, which ends:

> And the sunset bath'd in the gulf to lend her
> A garland of pinks and of purples tender,
> A tinge of the sun-god's rosy splendour,
>   A tithe of his glories manifold.

The fourth stanza begins:

> Man's works are graven, cunning, and skilful
>   On earth, where his tabernacles are;
> But the sea is wanton, the sea is wilful,
>   And who shall mend her and who shall mar?

It continues in this vein through eight stanzas, and closes with two stanzas of pure description, returning at the close to the mood in which it began.

Undeniably Gordon both felt and communicated an emotional response to nature. But it was a qualified response and a balanced response. There was joy in it, and also something corres-

ponding to sorrow. That is, there was the recognition that nature
was not all sunshine and gladness. He had none of that trust in
nature that the early Wordsworth had before his brother was
drowned at sea. Gordon is nearer to Byron.

One further point remains. There was an aspect of nature toward which his response was singleminded. He loved horses,
though, but since the horses were sooner or later trained and
domesticated by man, they were not wholly a part of nature.
Horses were his great love throughout his life:

> Yet if man, of all the Creator plann'd,
>   His noblest work is reckoned,
> Of the works of His hand, by sea or by land,
>   The horse may at least rank second.

So he wrote in the First Part of "Hippodromania." This emotion
was one which never left him. It is reflected throughout the
racing poems, but finds its most striking expression in "The Roll
of the Kettledrum; or, The Lay of the Last Charger." In this
poem it is the horse who is the speaker. He recalls to mind the
part he played in the Charge of the Light Brigade. Then his
mind in engaged by the figure of the old Colonel, who is lonely,
so lonely that as he finally turns away his last words are, "Would
to God I had died with your master, old man!" Gordon attributes
to the horse a lively sympathy with man and man's sorrows, and
rationalizes the attribution:

> The wide gulf that parts us may yet be no wider
>   Than that which parts you from some being more blest;
> And there may be more links 'twixt the horse and his rider
>   That ever your shallow philosophy guess'd.

Emotion is also attached, sometimes, to abstract ideas and
ideals. Patriotism is the most common of these, and it is absent
from Gordon's poetry. Australians in his day and for a good
while thereafter were not particularly patriotic. They did not
display a political love of country. They may have loved their
country as a place to live, and as the locale of their families and
friends (although they tended more than Canadians to keep
emotional ties with "home") but they did not have much feeling
for "Queen and country." In fact, the Sydney *Bulletin* in the
1890's, a generation later than Gordon, was to print comments
on the home government and the Royal family which would have
invited prosecution if they had been published elsewhere in the

English-speaking world.[3] The day of the Anzacs and of the National War Memorial was then still in the future. Australia had no political nationhood, and (an important point) no foreign enemy to fear.

There was a Canadian verse-maker who wrote, in Gordon's lifetime:

> Once more is the flag of old Britain unfurl'd,
>   And flauntingly kisses the wind;
> Her foe is a despot, the scourge of the world,
>   Her cause is the rights of mankind.[4]

Gordon was both too much of a realist and too much of a poet to have written anything like this. His patriotism was concrete, not abstract. The reference in Fytte VIII of "Ye Wearie Wayfarer" to "the chimes of· sweet St. Mary's / On far English ground" gives us a rare look into feelings for his early homeland which he normally concealed or seldom allowed himself to feel. The feelings were for the sights and sounds of the country, not for its flag or its political arrangements.

Nor did he show any enthusiasm for such concepts as liberty or equality. He had all the liberty he needed, and as a policeman his concern had been for law and order. He had enough sense to realize that liberty is impossible without law and order, but he made no point of it. He had, as we have seen, no passion for the ideals of social reform. He did not burn to create a better society. Even in the concrete he did not pity the plight of the poor. He liked the poor, when he liked them at all, just as they were.

The ideals of courage and kindliness aroused a response in his poetry, even as abstractions, but poetry cannot be made out of abstractions. When he had said that "kindness" and "courage" are things that "stand like stone," he had gone as far as the abstractions would take him.

The concrete images of courage that went into his poetry were a different matter. They were a part of his main emotional response, what we have called the "love of life." It was really a love of one side of life only, the muscular side which belonged to the out-of-doors and "God's glorious oxygen." Like the other positive emotions, it involves both joy and sorrow—joy when the emotion brings fulfillment and sorrow when it is faced with loss or frustration.

Both sides are present in "The Roll of the Kettledrum." The

poem is a highly charged emotional presentation of contrasting
themes of life and death. The emotion of life, the thrill of being
alive, is heightened by the presence of death, which is heightened
in turn in two ways. The death that threatens is dramatic. It is
not mere death, but death by violence; it is not mere death by
violence, but death in battle. The battle is the most dramatic
kind of battle. It is a cavalry charge, for one thing, and for another, to the reader who recognizes the connotations of the story,
it is a charge against hopeless odds. These are fighters who, like
Cyrano de Bergerac, do not fight always to win. It is the spice of
danger that gives life its value.

The last line of the twenty-first stanza, which ends the first
half of the poem, is the significant one: "He was never more
happy in life than in death." This is the opinion of the "last
charger," but there is no doubt that Gordon meant this, and
meant us to feel that his hero was happy in his death because he
had been happy in life, that he had taken all his risks gladly, and
that he had "died game" and therefore died well.

The line is glossed by a passage near the end of Fytte II of
"Ye Wearie Wayfarer":

> I remember the laugh that all the while
>   On his quiet features played:—
> So he rode to his death, with that careless smile,
>   In the van of the "Light Brigade;"
>
> So stricken by Russian grape, the cheer
>   Rang out, while he toppled back,
> From the shattered lungs as merry and clear
>   As it did when it roused the pack.

The negative side of this emotion makes the theme of the second half of the poem. The old colonel envies the early death of
Nolan.[5] The colonel also has loved life in all its aspects, and has
lost it through the passage of time. Age has enfeebled his body
and has robbed him of his family by death or disgrace. Taking
the poem as a whole, we have to admit that the emphasis is on
this negative side, for three reasons. First, the second half of the
poem is longer than the first, by twenty-nine stanzas to twenty-
one. Secondly, the final climax of the poem is the colonel's regret
for not having died young. Thirdly, the title of the poem refers
to the poem's ending rather than to the battle scene; the roll of
the kettledrum in the last stanza is an accompaniment to the
colonel's final speech.

This duality, and this balance, of emotion runs right through Gordon's poetry, with one apparent exception. The joy of life goes along with the acceptance of death and the risk of death. When death crowns life with honor, it is to be embraced. When life goes on too long, the joy of living is replaced by the sorrow of outliving what has made life worthwhile. The exception is "The Sick Stockrider," who, unlike the colonel in "The Roll of the Kettledrum," is able to rejoice in the thought of the activities and friendships of the past. Elsewhere, the emotional pattern is adjusted to this proposition: life is to be rejoiced in while it is bold and free and active, but unless it is crowned by early death the joy will turn to sorrow, and to the conclusion which Browning uncharacteristically stated in his depression after the death of Miss Egerton Smith, "Sorrow did, and joy did nowise—life well weighed—preponderate."[6]

III *Fear and Anger*

The negative emotions of fear and anger hold a less prominent place in poetry than the positive ones of joy and sorrow. This is specially true of the emotion of fear. It is found in dramatic poetry, most notably in Book XI of Browning's *The Ring and the Book;* it is not often to be found in lyric poetry which is, or may be taken for, the expression of the poet's own feelings. There is an obvious reason for this. Fear is the least creditable of all emotions. No one but an adolescent is ashamed of being in love or of being deeply affected by bereavement, but we are ashamed of being afraid.

Gordon had no fears to express, in the ordinary sense of the term. He was either born without fear, or he suppressed the emotion so consistently, resisting it by doing the things that he might have been afraid of, that the result was the same. And the characters of his narratives are mostly without fear, romantic dashing heroes, or (as in "Wolf and Hound") hard-working un-imaginative men doing their duty, for whom fear seems to have no meaning.

In this, Gordon was a Victorian and not a modern. The fear-less soldier was a Victorian image; or rather, the fearless officer was a Victorian image. The private soldiers, or the ordinary sea-men of the Royal Navy, might have to be kept to their duty by fear of brutal punishments, but the officers were supposed to be above all fear. Even Kipling's realism does not disturb this pic-ture. In the twentieth century our image of the soldier is that of

the man who does his duty while he is frightened and in spite
of being frightened. It is less glamorous, but more true, and, in
its way, more impressive.[7]

One form of fear is respectable when it is kept in moderation.
That is the fear of the cosmos, and of the awesome aspects of
the natural universe. We commonly describe it as "awe," and it
is not really an emotion of fear so much as an aesthetic response.
Allied with this is a sense of awe in the face of the uncertainty
of life's meaning and purpose and also of the fact of death. The
first two of these find their way into "Cui Bono," only to be dis-
missed with a shrug at the end of the stanza:

> The wail of the breeze in the bending trees
>   Is something between a laugh and a groan;
> And the hollow roar of the surf on the shore
>   Is a dull, discordant monotone;
> I wish I could guess what sense they express,
>   There's a meaning, doubtless, in every sound,
> Yet no one can tell, and it may be as well—
>   Whom would it profit?—The world goes round!

Something of the same awe at the destructive power of nature
governs "The Song of the Surf," and a corresponding feeling
about the "human predicament" is in "Wormwood and Nightshade," epitomized by the eleventh stanza:

> The restless throbbings and burnings
>   That hope unsatisfied brings,
> The weary longings and yearnings
>   For the mystical better things,
> Are the sands on which is reflected
>   The pitiless moving lake,
> Where the wanderer falls dejected
>   By a thirst he never can slake.

It was mainly the sea which roused these emotions in Gordon.
We see them again in "The Swimmer," along with an expression
of the fear of death in the only form which he would admit. The
first is best exemplified from the fourth stanza:

> Man's works are graven, cunning, and skilful
>   On earth where his tabernacles are;
> But the sea is wanton, the sea is wilful,
>   And who shall mend her and who shall mar?
> Shall we carve success or record disaster

> On her bosom of heaving alabaster?
> Will her purple pulse beat fainter or faster
> For fallen sparrow or fallen star?

The second comes into the tenth stanza:

> A little season of love and laughter,
> Of light and life, and pleasure and pain,
> And a horror of outer darkness after,
> And dust returneth to dust again.

There is a relatively respectable fear, which is the fear of disgrace. This is the central emotion of "Ten Paces Off (Scene XI of the "Road to Avernus" sequence), which has already been discussed in another connection.[8] This will be clear if we repeat the central lines:

> Though God will never forgive me,
> Though men make light of my name,
> Though my sin and my shame outlive me,
> I shall not outlast my shame.

If we think about these lines in their context, we shall see that there are two fears here, and that the one on the surface is not the important one. What Laurence seems to fear is disgrace in the eyes of other men. But the trick which his friend has devised is at least not certain to be detected, and has apparently been worked at least once before. What Laurence really fears is himself. He would not be able to live with himself, knowing that he had killed his man unfairly, and he rejects the opportunity. His fear of standing low in his own opinion is stronger than his fear of death.

Since Homer's treatment of the wrath of Achilles, anger has taken only a little larger place in poetry than fear. When it does, at least in the last two centuries, it has taken the form of "righteous anger," directed against some evil, or unfairness, or social injustice. Burns fulminated in verse against the narrowness and hypocrisy of the Auld Lichts, and Shelley against the reactionary goverment of his day in "The Masque of Anarchy" and the "Song to the Men of England." Tennyson, through the speakers in "Locksley Hall" and *Maud,* expressed his anger at certain aspects of the attitudes of Victorian England. In the United States, John G. Whittier, in "Ichabod"—though he wrote more in sorrow than in anger—said what he thought about Daniel Webster's support of the Clay Compromise of 1850.

Gordon did not strike any of these attitudes. He was not an angry young man. As we have seen, he did not resent the injustices of his society, nor the inhuman class distinctions of the nineteenth-century world, as Henry Lawson was to do later. His own troubles did not rouse him to anger. He gets no nearer to it than the hints in early poems written at the time of his exile. The reference to his mother as "a stately dame" in " 'Early Adieux,' " and to the girl whose breast was "very near as cold" as snow, are suggestions of a resentment that he did not bring out into the open, but they are no more than that. In the poem "No Name" the second stanza is:

> I said in my wrath, when his shadow cross'd
> From your garden gate to your cottage door,
> "What does it matter for one soul lost,
> Millions of souls have been lost before."

E. M. Robb's Note identifies the "you" of the poem with Jane Bridges, but the identification is exceedingly remote. Gordon has taken a few memories of his own early experience as a starting point, and has built around them a story quite different from his own. The "wrath" belongs to the story, not to Gordon.

One other poem is supposed to be related to Gordon's emotional life, and presumably to the story of Jane Bridges. It is called " 'The Old Leaven' (A Dialogue)" and was not included in any of the books published by Gordon but was added later to the collected editions. Mr. and Mrs. T. H. Ilbury, in the *Western Australia Historical Society Journal and Proceedings*, Vol. I, Part 2 (1928), in the course of a very useful account of Gordon's trip to Western Australia, state categorically that the poem was autobiographical, and was written by Gordon just before he left on that unlucky expedition. The dialogue is between Mark and Maurice, Maurice representing Gordon—if either does. Mark begins:

> So, Maurice, you sail to-morrow, you say?
> And you may or may not return?
> Be sociable, man! for once in a way,
> Unless you're too old to learn.

Maurice is in a bad mood, and Mark is trying to find out why. Maurice rejects several suggestions, but when Mark hazards the guess that "That girl that jilted you long ago, / You're thinking of her, confess!" Maurice admits that it is so.

Maurice admits to anger, and Mark is conscious of it. Mark urges him to "Be a Christian for once, not a Pagan Turk, / Nursing wrath and keeping it warm." (How long since Gordon had read "Tam O'Shanter"?) He elaborates his good advice:

> She's a matron now; when you knew her first
>   She was but a child, and your hate,
> Fostered and cherished, nourished and nursed,
>   Will it ever evaporate?
> Your grievance is known to yourself alone,
>   But, Maurice, I say, for shame,
> If in ten long years you haven't outgrown
>   Ill-wind to an ancient flame.

Maurice admits that he has spoken "in spite" and now will lay his ill-will aside:

> Against her no word from my lips shall pass,
>   Betraying the grudge I've cherished,
> Till the sand runs down in my hour-glass,
>   And the gift of my speech has perished.

The ending is characteristically Gordon:

> *Maurice (yawning):*
> Who knows? not I; I can hardly vouch
>   For the truth of what little I see;
> And, now, if you've any weed in your pouch,
>   Just hand it over to me.

There are three possible ways of taking this. One is that it really is autobiographical and that it really refers to Jane Bridges. If this is so, then he did have a bitter and long-standing anger against her, which he finally works out thirteen years after his jilting and four years after his marriage to Maggie Park. It is possible, but not likely in view of the tone in which he mentioned Jane in one of his early letters from South Australia. Moreover, it is a fact of human nature that we are angry only when we have the feeling that some right of ours has been infringed. We are not angry at the man who steps on our feet on a crowded bus, so long as we feel that he could not help it; we grow angry when we feel that he could have avoided the accident if he had been more careful. It is hard on Gordon to suppose that in all these years he had not realized that he had no right to expect Jane to accept his sudden proposal, blurted out at an awkward moment and with no preliminary attentions to lead up to it.

The second interpretation is that the poem refers to some affair of Gordon's which happened during his years as a horse-breaker and of which we have no independent knowledge. If we assume that the poem was written on the eve of his departure for Western Australia, and if we take literally Mark's reference to "ten long years," we must suppose that the event took place in 1856, just after his leaving the Mounted Police and before his first meeting with Father Woods. The best we can say is that it could have been so.

Two factual statements in the poem bear on this question. The first is:

> I saw my lady the other night
>   In the crowded opera hall,
> When the boxes sparkled with faces bright,
>   I knew her amongst them all.

This rules out Jane, if we take it seriously, and it probably rules out any local, South Australian belle too. It is impossible to believe that Gordon in 1856 would have been making advances to any lady likely to be found, then or thereafter, among the boxes at the opera. It tells us that if there is any autobiographical element worth considering in the poem, it has been altered and dressed up a good deal. The second such statement is:

> Time was when to pleasure her girlish whim,
>   In my blind infatuation,
> I've freely endangered life and limb;
>   Aye, perilled my soul's salvation.

This does not rule out the hypothetical Australian girl, but it practically rules out Jane. Nothing in what we know of the relation between them suggests any such showing off to "pleasure her girlish whim." It would be safer to say that until the day of his proposal he hardly knew what her girlish whims were.

The third interpretation is that Gordon is making up a scene, with a story behind it; that in so doing he has used an experience of his own, but that he has altered both the facts and the emotions to suit a poetic purpose not in the least autobiographical.

We arrive at this conclusion, that there is very little of the negative emotions of fear and anger in Gordon's poems, and that this absence is closely related to his life and character. He was never afraid, and rarely angry.

CHAPTER 7

Technics and Influences

POETRY, in the full sense of the word, is in verse, and the essence of verse is its metric pattern, which in English verse is a rhythmic pattern. The metric "foot"—whether we think of it in the classical terms of "iamb," "trochee," or "dactyl," or whether we think in the more flexible terms needed for the rhythms of G. M. Hopkins and T. S. Eliot—remains the protoplasmic unit of which poetry is constructed. Rhythms are fundamental. The superstructure includes the decorative devices of rhyme, assonance, and alliteration; the diction selected; the patterns of imagery if they are significant; and the use of figures of speech from the simile to the symbolic metaphor.

I *The Basic Form*

In general terms, the conspicuous fact about the metrics of English poetry is the apparent predominance of the pentameter line. This predominance is stronger in appearance than in reality. To settle the question would involve a tedious statistical analysis. Without the statistics, one simply remembers that eight-ninths of *The Faerie Queene*, all of *Paradise Lost*, practically all of Shakespeare, the whole of *The Prelude, The Idylls of the King*, and *The Ring and the Book*, not to mention the couplets of Chaucer, Dryden, Pope, and of Keat's *Endymion*, are written in the pentameter, or five-stress, line. In short, the pentameter line has been the norm for serious English poetry, from the fourteenth century to the end of the nineteenth.

As a rule, though far from an invariable one, the shorter lines are found in works of smaller scale or of less seriousness. Milton's Companion Pieces are by no means trivial, but they obviously have less weight, less intensity, and less sense of purpose than *Lycidas* or *Comus*. Scott used tetrameter couplets for *The Lady of the Lake,* a romance in which the interest is entirely narrative. Tennyson used shorter lines for his earlier, experimental lyrics; for the classical poems and for *The Idylls of the King* he chose the pentameter. The principal exception in Tennyson's poetry is itself instructive. *In Memoriam* is probably the only full-scale, major, serious poem in English written in tetrameters; and the success of the rhythm is evidence of Tennyson's technical skill, in that he was able to "slow" the tetrameter line enough to create harmony of form and mood.

The first fact to be noted, about Gordon's poetic technics, is that he almost never used the five-stress line. The two exceptions are of such a kind that the word "almost" is of little importance. The first is "Pastor Cum," a translation from Horace.[1] For this, he used pentameter lines with alternate rhyme, essentially the "elegiac stanza," though it is printed solidly throughout with no stanza-divisions. The second is in "The Sick Stockrider," where the even-numbered lines are five-stress lines. Of these two exceptions, the first, being a translation, is in a class by itself and the second, for obvious reasons, hardly counts at all.

So much for the line-unit which Gordon did not use: in order to examine what he did use, it is appropriate to begin with *Ashtaroth*, partly because it was his first book, in order of publication, but mainly because it presents the most complex problem. It is dramatic in form, and nearly one hundred pages long—one hundred and ten in the standard Oxford edition. The conventional form for dramatic verse in English is the unrhymed decasyllabic line. Even those poems which are but dramatic in form, and unsuited for the theater, commonly use this line for the body of the poem, as, for example, *Prometheus Unbound* or *Atalanta in Calydon* or Byron's *Manfred*. In such dramatic poems, other verse forms are mostly used for choruses, songs, and incantations. The pentameter line is the standard, to be departed from for the sake of special effects, or for variety.

Gordon does not use the pentameter line; his basic rhythm is the tetrameter. The first two scenes are in what is frequently called the "ballad stanza," the quatrain in which the first and third lines are of four stresses, and the second and fourth of three, with alternate rhyme. Gordon makes one difference. Whereas the conventional ballad stanza is rhymed *a b c b*, Gordon rhymes *a b a b*. Also, the lines are not printed as stanzas but in solid blocks of verse, except for Orion's song in the first scene, which is printed in eight-line units. The third scene is in a Swinburnean anapaestic trimeter (most of the lines beginning with an iambic foot), printed in eight-line stanzas rhyming *a b a b c d c d*. "Thora's Song," which begins the fourth scene, continues the same form; the remainder of the scene is in four-stress lines (the rhythm ,being a mixture of iambic and anapaestic) with alternate rhyme. The fifth scene is in tetrameter couplets, with a song at the end in six-line stanzas, rhyming *a b a a a b,* with the *b* lines in three stresses and the rest in four. The next two scenes are in the ballad-stanza form, with several lines divided between speeches, and another song at the close of the seventh scene, again in anapaestic trimeter. The eighth scene is made up of six-line units, mostly printed in longer blocks. The rhyme is *a a b c c b;* the *b* lines have six stresses each, and the others three.

It would be tedious and unnecessary to continue the inspection. The metric structure of the poem is sufficiently clear. The basic meter is tetrameter, varied in different ways by the use of trimeter lines. The form of the ballad stanza is frequently used, and tetrameter couplets a little more so. Two-stress lines are used occasionally; the twenty-fifth scene is in this form throughout. The key word for the poem's metrics is "variety," which is, to do it justice, skillfully managed. The proof of this is in the fact that it does not become tedious—not, that is, in this way or for this reason. Nothing is more monotonous than constant change, or more tiresome than change clumsily handled.

In the poems which make up the two principal volumes, the four-stress line is the most frequent. The ballad stanza is rarely used, and generally with some variations presently to be considered. The first two poems in *Sea Spray and Smoke Drift* are both in tetrameters, with alternate rhyme. "Ye Wearie Way-farer" is in the ballad stanza, although not printed in quatrains but in groups of eight lines, and sometimes of twelve or more. The same is true of most of the early pieces, such as "To My Sister," and, of course, *The Feud.* It is necessary to look more closely at the rhythms and stanza forms which Gordon used.

II *The Rhythms Used*

The question of stanza form is inseparable from that of rhyme, and not easily separable from that of rhythm. These three matters, therefore, have to be considered, or reconsidered, together. The first general statement to be made is that Gordon always wrote in stanzas, even in those few poems in which he may appear at first sight not to have done so.

Sea Spray and Smoke Drift shows a good deal of variety, as one would expect. The variety, however, is limited. The predominance of the four-stress line warns us of that. It remains to notice what a range of difference Gordon was able to produce within the technical limitation of the four-stress line. The first two poems in the book give an introductory sample of the differences.

"Podas Okus" is written in that ambiguous rhythm which is fairly common in English verse: it could be scanned as either iambic or trochaic. If iambic, the first foot of each line is defective, since every line begins with a stressed syllable; if trochaic, the final feet of half the lines are defective, since every even-numbered line ends in a stressed syllable. The only valid test is the reader's ear and taste. On this ground, and because the odd-numbered lines are regular trochaic, we shall consider the rhythm of the whole as trochaic, or a "falling accent." We thus have this pattern of scansion:

$$/ \ x \ / \ x \ / \ x \ / \ x$$
$$/ \ x \ / \ x \ / \ x \ /$$

The rhythm is consistently followed throughout, in eight-line stanzas, with the rhyme *a b a b c d c d*. The odd-numbered lines all have feminine rhyme. Variety within the poem is secured by the shift of caesural pauses, and by a sparse use of the pyrrhic foot and a still more sparse use of the spondee.

The second poem, "Gone," is also in tetrameters, and in eight-line stanzas with alternate rhyme, but the rhythmic effect is quite different. Instead of the falling accent of the trochaic line, there is a rising accent; whether we call it iambic with a mixture of anapaests, or anapaestic with a mixture of iambuses, is optional. Two lines out of sixty-four have an extra, unstressed syllable at the end, making a feminine rhyme, or half-rhyme ("water" and "shorter"). Seven lines begin with an unmistakably stressed syllable; of these some must, and all may, be considered as defective opening feet. The first four lines are adequate as examples:

$$x \ / \quad x \ x \quad / \quad x \ x \ / \quad x \ /$$
In Col | lins Street stand | eth a sta | tue tall—
$$x \ / \quad x \ / \quad x \ x \ / \quad x \ x \ /$$
A sta | tue tall | on a pil | lar of stone,
$$/ \quad x \ x \ / \quad x \ x \ / \quad x \ /$$
Tell | ing its sto | ry, to great | and small,
$$x \ x \quad / \quad x \ / \quad x \ x \ / \quad / \quad /$$
Of the dust | reclaimed | from the sand | waste lone.

The first Fytte of "Ye Wearie Wayfarer" shows the same essential rhythm with a different stanza. There is the alternation of four-stress and three-stress lines characteristic of the ballad stanza; though to the eye there are two stanzas of twelve lines each, there are in fact six stanzas of ballad rhythm. The metric scheme of the first four lines is:

```
/ | x x / | x x / | / /
    x / | x x / | x /
x x / | x / | x x / | x /
    x / | x x / | x /
```

As usual with Gordon, the odd-numbered lines rhyme as well as the even-numbered ones.

The second Fytte introduces a variation, the same device as Coleridge used to give variety to "The Ancient Mariner." In two places there are added four-stress lines, with adjacent rhyme. The ninth to the fifteenth lines are rhymed *a b a a b a b*; the *a* lines are tetrameter, the *b* lines trimeter. The same device is used in the fourth and fifth Fyttes.

In the eighth and final Fytte, "Finis Exoptatus," the rhythm changes. Now we have the trochaic, or "falling accent." Except that half the lines are trimeters rather than tetrameters, the rhythm is identical with that of "Podas Okus"; there are the same feminine rhymes in the odd-numbered lines, and the same defective final feet in the even-numbered lines. The rhythm suits the mood. The second best-known lines in the poem follow the pattern with perfect regularity:

```
      /    x    /    x    / x  |/  x
• Hark! the | bells on | distant | cattle
      /    x'   /      x    /
    Waft a | cross the | range,
      /      x   /   x    /  x   /  x
    Through the | golden | -tufted | wattle
      /   x   /   x      /
    Music | low and | strange.
```

The best-known lines of all, if they are rightly read, illustrate his use of the pyrrhic foot.

```
      /  x  /  x     /   x    /  x
    Life is | mostly | froth and | bubble,
      /     x     /     x    /
    Two things | stand like | stone—
```

/   x   x   x   / x   / x
KINDNESS | in an | other's | trouble,
/   x   / x   x | /
COURAGE | in your | own.

This same trochaic rhythm appears again in "A Legend of Madrid," with a more·complex stanza and with four-stress lines throughout. There are sixteen lines to a stanza, and the rhyme is *a b a b c d c d e e e f g g g f;* the *a, c, e,* and *g* lines are in feminine rhyme. There are nine stanzas, and two of them are divided between the two speakers, Nina and Francesca. Otherwise all is neat and regular, except for the twelfth line of the third stanza ("To the muleteer's child."), which is reduced to a trimeter. This gives emphasis to an important fact—indeed, the central fact in Francesca's mind and in her emotions.

A similiar speculation arises from a close look at the stanzas of "Rippling Water." The lines are again four-stressed, iambic with a plentiful sprinkling of anapaests, and organized in stanzas of twelve lines. The first stanza is rhymed *a b a b a a a b c d c d.* So is the second, with, of course, a new set of rhymes. But in the third the rhyme becomes *a b a b c c c b d e d e;* that is, lines five to seven use a new rhyme instead of repeating the rhyme of lines two and four. It looks as if Gordon had found it too difficult to provide five rhymes for each stanza, and had simplified his problem when he came to stanza three. However, in the last two stanzas, the sixth and the seventh, he returns to the original rhyme. Did he get a kind of "second wind"? Or did he arrange it so on purpose? The symmetry of it suggests the second possibility; the first two and the last two stanzas are in one form, and the middle three in a slightly different form. If he did it on purpose, what was his purpose? Here again, the important question gets no answer.

Two of the poems, "Unshriven" and "Cui Bono," make good use of internal rhyme. "Cui Bono" is printed in straightforward tetrameters, and in twelve-line stanzas; in effect, it might be considered as two dimeter lines to each tetrameter, rhyming *a a b c c b.* "Unshriven" presents a special problem in metrics, to be considered later.

Bush Ballads and Galloping Rhymes needs little further comment. There are fewer poems than in the earlier volume, and a narrower range of prosodic variety. The four-stress line is predominant, and the mixed rhythm, anapaestic and iambic, continues to appear. One poem, however, provides an interesting problem in prosody.

If "The Sick Stockrider" be examined according to conventional principles, it is found to be written in heptameter and pentameter iambic lines. In the slow-moving opening section, this is the actual rhythm.

x / x / x / x / x / x
Hold hard, | Ned! lift | me down | once more, | and lay | me

x x /
in | the shade;

x / x / x / x / x /
Old man, | you've had | your work | cut out | to guide. . . .

With the second section, at line twenty-one, the rhythm quickens, and the lines may be read as four-stressed and three-stressed:

x / x x x / x x x / x x x
'Twas mer | ry in the glow | ing morn, among | the gleaming

/
grass,

x / x x x / x x x /
To wan | der as we've wan | der'd many a mile.

This scansion is a little misleading. What really happens is that each of the extended feet has a secondary stress, making the true pattern x // x / , which is analogous to "common," or "4/4," time in music. Further on in the poem, especially in the lines beginning "In these hours when life is ebbing," there are passages which can be read in the conventional fashion, with seven and five stresses. At the very end, however, the lighter rhythm becomes hard to avoid.

x x / x x x / x x x / x
Let me slum | ber in the hol | low where the wat | tle

x x /
blossoms wave,

x / x x x / x x x /
With ne | ver stone or rail | to fence my bed;

x x / x x x / x x x /
Should the stur | dy station child | ren pull the bush |

x x x /
flowers on my grave,

x x / x x x / x x x /
I may chance | to hear them romp | ing overhead.

The quiet, almost light-hearted, acceptance of death could scarcely be more subtly or more effectively conveyed.

This rhythm had been used earlier for "Unshriven," in *Sea Spray and Smoke Drift*. The stanzas have four lines each, but there is internal rhyme, so that the pattern of rhyme and rhythm becomes:

```
x x / x x x /              a
x x / x x x /              a
x / x x x / x x x / b
x x / x x x /              c
x x / x x x /              c
x / x x x / x x x / b
```

At first blush, this seems a less successful, less justifiable, use of an unusual rhythm. The lightness of the verse seems in contradiction to the heavy mood of a tale of sudden death. On the other hand, there is contrast made explicit in the words of the poem. The opening line, "Oh! the sun rose on the lea, and the bird sang merrilie," is repeated twice more, with slight changes, within less than thirty lines. The contrast between the gaiety of nature and the happiness of marriage ("We were wed but yesternoon") on one side, and the violent death of the bridegroom on the other is the very stuff of the poem. When technic reinforces and harmonizes with content, judgment in its favor may be demanded.

III   Rhyme, and Other Adornments

Gordon's ear for rhyme can be called in question. Certainly a *prima facie* case can be made out against him. In "Bellona" (*Sea Spray and Smoke Drift*), he rhymes "archangel" with "strangle," "forth" with "path" and "wrath," "shapely" with "rape lie," and "harness" with "scorn is." In "A Legend of Madrid," he rhymes "sombrero" with "hero," "lady" with "shade I," "Madonna" with "honour," and "head lie" with "redly" and "deadly." In "From the Wreck," he rhymes "cross" with "horse," "swamp" with "Camp," and "spurs" with "ears." In his defense there are two points to be made. First, something must be allowed for differences and changes in pronunciation. In English speech—the speech, that is, of England—"forth" sounds more like "wrath," and "Madonna" more like "honour," than in most forms of American speech. In Scene XI of "The Road to Avernus," "Prescot" is rhymed with "waistcoat"; to an Englishman this would sound like a perfect rhyme, whereas to an American, who would probably prounounce the second word like "wastecoat," it would not. Secondly, it may be urged as a plea in mitigation that half-rhymes are used and accepted in poetry. The poems of Emily Dickinson, for example, are well supplied with them, and she was a contemporary of Gordon's, although her poems did not come before the public until after her death. Still, when all is said, it must be admitted that Gordon did not achieve perfection in rhyming; but the fault, considered in context, is venial, not mortal.

He had a penchant for feminine rhyme. In *Sea Spray and Smoke Drift,* half of the poems have feminine rhyme, generally in half of the lines. In *Bush Ballads and Galloping Rhymes,* of twenty poems (counting the sections of "The Road to Avernus" separately) there are eight that are similarly characterized. On the other hand, he was not much given to the kind of elaborate, or "forced" rhyme associated with Byron or Browning. He wrote always in rhyme, and with lots of rhyme. Even his use of the ballad stanza has the odd-numbered lines rhyming. And as a rule, with the qualifications already given, his rhymes were sound and satisfying.

Alliteration is the opposite to rhyme. Fundamental to Old English versification, it is in modern poetry a decorative feature, most effective when it is unobtrusive. With Gordon, it generally is unobtrusive, as in these lines from "Fauconshawe":

> Night black and chill, wind gathering still,
>   With its wail in the turret tall,
> And its headlong blast like a catapult cast,
>   On the crest of the outer wall.

It was not, to speak truth, always so. The alliteration is more conspicuous in the final lines of "Hippodromania":

> Since again from the earth his effulgence
>   The darkness and damp-dews shall wipe,
> Kind reader, extend your indulgence
>   To this the last lay of "The Pipe."

The first two stanzas of "A Dedication" are too well known to need quoting. Where alliteration becomes conspicuous in Gordon's verse, there is usually a perceptible influence of Swinburne.

The management of vowel sounds is a significant part of poetic technic. Some poetry can be classified as vocalic or consonantal. A good deal of Browning and of Kipling is consonantal, while Tennyson is characteristically vocalic. Speaking loosely, vowels give beauty to the verse and consonants give meaning.

One of Gordon's earliest poems, "To My Sister" (1853), begins:

> Across the trackless seas I go,
>   No matter when or where,
> And few my future lot will know,
>   And fewer still will care.

In these lines the vowel-play is not memorable, nor do the consonants contribute anything except their bare function of shaping
sounds. into sense. Gordon has expressed a predictable emotion
in an unobjectionable but undistinguished fashion. He has
achieved pathos without bathos, and that is all.

If we turn to the closing lines of "The Rhyme of Joyous Garde,"
we find a different effect.

> When the world as a wither'd leaf shall be,
> And the sky like a shrivell'd scroll shall flee,
> And souls shall be summon'd from land and sea,
>   At the blast of His bright archangel.

The preponderance of long vowels (and two diphthongs), the
use of short vowels mainly in the unimportant words, the assonance in the first two lines, and the supporting use of semi-vowels,
sibilants, and liquid consonants, all work together to bring the
poem to a technically satisfactory conclusion. Indeed, these
effects are sufficient to conceal the sextuple alliteration in the
second and third lines, so that the reader is hardly conscious of
it unless he stops to count, which is as it should be.

One would hardly expect technical subtleties in "The Sick
Stockrider," but they are there. The opening lines are marked by
long vowels and diphthongs, and by stopped consonants which
help to slow the rhythm. The closing lines are made up chiefly of
short vowels, but many of them are "long by position," as the
rule for Latin scansion has it. Between the beginning and the
end are the lines: "With a running fire of stockwhips and a fiery
run of hoofs, / Oh! the hardest day was never then too hard!"
The interplay of vowels, long and short, with nasal and liquid
consonants give the necessary swiftness to the lines, while the
stopped consonants give the "snap" which the image calls for.

IV *Imagery*

Poetry is compounded of images, mediated to the imagination
by memorable words structured in patterns. Of Gordon's images
there is not much that can usefully be said. There is nothing in
his verse comparable to "the morn, in russet mantle clad / Walks
o'er the dew of yon high eastern hills." The only question to be
asked is: Are there any images that seem characteristic, or
typical, or repeated?

The landscape-images, and weather-images, are usually somber and forbidding. In "Cui Bono" we have "wind that whistles,"

"wail of the breeze," and "the hollow roar of the surf." "From Lightning and Tempest" gives us images both of storm and of plague, when the men's "bloom was a ghastly pallor, and their smile was a ghastly frown." In "Wormwood and Nightshade" we read that

> The rays of the sunset redden
>   With a sullen and lurid frown,
> From the skies that are dark and leaden,
>   To earth that is dusk and brown.

The first part of "Hippodromania," which begins cheerily enough, ends with similar images, as "The neutral tint of the sullen sea / Is flecked with the snowy foam." The opening landscape of "De Te" creates the same effect, though implicitly rather than explicitly.

> A burning glass of burnish'd brass,
>   The calm sea caught the noontide rays,
> And sunny slopes of golden grass
>   And wastes of weed-flower seem'd to blaze.
> . . . .
> We heard the hound beneath the mound,
>   We scared the swamp hawk hovering nigh—
> We had not sought for that we found—
>   He lay as dead men only lie.

That Gordon's poetry is well supplied with images of death, mostly violent, hardly requires to be demonstrated.

Color-imagery is dominated by red. "Podas Okus" has "crimson sand," "Scamander's torrent red," and "red lips," as well as "golden sunset," "violet orbs," "amber tresses," and "golden rain." Add to these "redder than dews at eventide" ("Gone"), "red horizon" ("Ye Wearie Wayfarer, Fytte VIII"), "blood-red scarf" ("A Legend of Madrid"), "blood-red her nostrils" ("From the Wreck"), "whose banner floats blood-red" ("Ashtaroth," scene seventeen)—these are sufficient samples. Gold is prominent; the milder colors, blue, green, and pink occur infrequently.

Images of battle and of weapons are plentiful. *Sea Spray and Smoke Drift* begins, almost, with

> Doubtful strain of desp'rate battle,
>   Cut and thrust and grapple fierce,
> Swords that ring on shields that rattle,
>   Blades that gash and darts that pierce;—

and ends with the "streak of blue sword-blades all bared for the fleshing" of "The Roll of the Kettledrum." In Part IV of "Hippodromania," in describing a race, he writes: "In the van of the battle I heard the logs rattle, / His stroke never seem'd to diminish." The word "battle," though appropriate for a football match, is less so for a race, but it provides a convenient rhyme to "rattle," and more significantly derives from Gordon's fiercely competitive spirit. It is reinforced by the word "stroke," which, because of the proximity of "battle," takes on overtones of swordplay. Perhaps the finest of such structures of imagery is that of the thirtieth stanza of "The Rhyme of Joyous Garde":

> And the long lithe sword in the hand became
> As a leaping light, as a falling flame,
>   As a fire through the flax that hasted;
> Slender, and shining, and beautiful,
> How it shore through shivering casque and skull,
> And never a stroke was void and null,
>   And never a thrust was wasted.

It is to be supposed that Gordon's poetry would be richly supplied with the imagery of sport, but in fact there is less than we would look for. In Fytte IV of "Ye Wearie Wayfarer" there is an opening stanza on single-stick ("In the crossing guard, where the ash-plants kiss"), followed by brief and commonplace touches of cricket, football, hunting and fishing. Of boxing, there is practically nothing, anywhere, except "And hit out straight, 'tis your shortest plan, / When against the ropes you're driven." Horse-racing provides one image used in the same metaphorical way to point a moral, in the same Fytte: "And, whatever you do, don't change your mind / When once you have picked your panel." For the rest, images from the race-course are less prominent, quantitatively, than one might expect. *Si exempla requiris*, read "How We Beat the Favourite," or "Hippodromania."

V   *Influences*

Much has been made of the influences which are supposed to have shaped Gordon's verse, both in content and in style. The most elaborate treatment is by F. M. Robb, in his extensive Introduction to the standard edition of the poems.[2] Shelley, Byron, Browning, Tennyson, and Swinburne are all laid under contribution and all discussed at length.

There is considerable exaggeration in all this. Poets do, of course, imitate one another; so do painters, popular singers, acrobats, surgeons, and hairdressers. It may be that Gordon's tendency to give Latin titles to his poems ("Quare Fatigasti," "Cui Bono") is an imitation of Browning's similar use, as in "Tertium Quid" or "De Gustibus." To establish significant resemblances, however, it needs more than loose verbal similarities.

The influence of Byron on *Ashtaroth* need not be denied. Moreover, there are similarities deeper than story or style. Gordon had a distant blood-connection with the race of Byron, and something of Byron's melancholy. He had something of Byron's irresponsibility, but little of his cynicism and none of his exhibitionism. He did not publicly drag his bleeding heart across South Australia and Victoria.

The connection with Tennyson is much weaker. Gordon occasionally shows skill in onomatopoeia, as Robb has pointed out, but that device is in the public domain, and Gordon's use of it is not really comparable to Tennyson's. Gordon uses Arthurian material which he may well have got from Tennyson—or elsewhere—but in content and tone "The Rhyme of Joyous Garde" is nearer to William Morris than to Tennyson.

The influence of Browning is more controversial. In Fytte VII of "Ye Wearie Wayfarer" Gordon celebrates, briefly, "the wild joys of living"; also, the reference to Nolan links him with Browning's courage and so-called optimism. Gordon's courage, though, was in a different mood from Browning's. It was a stoic acceptance rather than a positive feeling that "we fall to rise, are baffled to fight better." The dominating mood was nearly always tinged with melancholy. There is a parallel between Gordon and Browning which has been generally overlooked. The line in "La Saisiaz," "Sorrow did and joy did nowise,—life well weighed,—preponderate," might be set beside the opening of Gordon's "Wormwood and Nightshade," "The troubles of life are many, / The pleasures of life are few." The trouble is that the, first quotation is, taken by itself, uncharacteristic of Browning whereas the second is characteristic of Gordon.

The parallels that have been drawn between specific poems seem forced. "Wolf and Hound" is not really much like "Childe Roland to the Dark Tower Came." There is some resemblance in the landscapes, a little (though much less) in the moods of the two heroes, and considerably more in the attitudes of the lying guides. But the stories are different in kind, the motivations are apparently different, and the endings are certainly different. The stanzas are different, the metrics are different, and the diction is different, as between the two poems. To suggest, as Robb does on page xcviii, that Gordon has made a "parable of the soul's aspiration and conquest" is pushing the matter much too hard for easy credibility. The comparison of "From the Wreck" with "How They Brought the Good News from Ghent to Aix" is more soundly based. The stories are alike and the rhythms are alike. The most that can be said on the other side is that given Gordon's interest in horses, his tendency to the use of anapaestic verse, and his having heard rumors of the rescue from *Admella*, he could have written his poem without necessarily having knowledge of, or hints from, Browning's. Since it is improbable in the extreme that he had not become familiar with Browning's poem, the point is a purely theoretical one.

In style the resemblance is very slight. Some of Gordon's odd rhymes are reminiscent of Browning's, as they are of Byron's and others'. Some of his phrasings might be matched from Browning's more conventional lyrics. Of the typical, recognizable, "Browning style," the style of "Fra Lippo Lippi," of "Saint Praxed's Church," or of "Blougram," there is practically nothing. Anyone who wishes to see what an imitation of Browning's style really looks like ought to read "One Viceroy Resigns," by Rudyard Kipling.

Swinburne is the poet whose influence on Gordon is most apparent. The chief mark of Swinburne's style is the use of repetitive devices, which take two principal forms. The first is alliteration (and assonance); the second is the sequence of similar words, phrases, or clauses, usually joined by "and" or "or," sometimes merely separated by commas. These are sufficiently exemplified in the fourth stanza of the first Chorus from *Atalanta in Calydon*:

> For winter's rains and ruins are over,
>   And all the season of snows and sins;
> The days dividing lover and lover,
>   The light that loses, the night that wins;
> And time remembered is grief forgotten,
> And frosts are slain and flowers begotten,
> And in green underwood and cover
>   Blossom by blossom the spring begins.

We have said that Gordon's alliteration is properly unobtrusive, with one qualification, which is that in those poems that have the stamp of Swinburne's influence on them the alliteration is more marked. Not only is it more frequent, but it is more con-

spicuous in relation to its frequency. Notice now the opening
lines of Gordon's "Bellona":

> Thou art moulded in marble impassive,
>   False goddess, fair statue of strife,
> Yet standest on pedestal massive,
>   A symbol and token of life.

A few lines further in the same poem we have this:

> Thy breath stirreth faction and party,
>   Men rise, and no voice can avail
> To stay them—rose-tinted Astarte
>   Herself at thy presence turns pale.

These lines are interesting because they show a bare minimum
of the specific devices that one can put a finger on; yet the experienced reader can hardly miss the aural idiom of Swinburnes-
que verse.

"The Song of the Surf," besides sharing Swinburne's feeling
for the sea, is written in the rhythm of "Hymn to Prosperpine"
and "Hesperia." It begins:

> White steeds of ocean, that leap with a hollow and
>   wearisome roar
> On the bar of ironstone steep, not a fathom's length
>   from the shore.

The specific tricks of repetition are less important than the effects
of rhythm and vowel-play. Nevertheless, these lines, and still
more the poem as a whole, clearly shows the Swinburnean touch,
which appears more explicitly in "The Swimmer":

> With short, sharp, violent lights made vivid,
>   To southward far as the sight can roam;
> Only the swirl of the surges livid,
>   The seas that climb and the surfs that comb.
> Only the crag and the cliff to nor'ward,
> And the rocks receding, and reefs flung forward,
> And waifs wreck'd seaward and wasted shoreward
>   On shallows sheeted with flaming foam.

Here we have just about the whole bag of tricks. Examples might
be multiplied, but not very far. Five of the poems—the three
already cited, plus "A Dedication" and "Doubtful Dreams"—

show clear, consistent Swinburnean influence. A few others show it in a state of dilution. The rest cannot properly be said to show it at all.

Influence has two aspects, the passive and the active. There are the influences by which a man is affected and there is the influence which he exerts. Gordon's active influence took three main forms.

First, he had some influence on the rise of the "bush-ballad" verse that reached a climax with Paterson and Lawson in the 1890's. How great, or how decisive, that influence was is open to question. There was a time when some appeared to regard him as the "onlie begetter" of the bush-ballad school. That time is past, partly because of the inevitable denigratory reaction (which in Gordon's case was relatively slow in getting under way) and partly because of scholarly investigation which has revealed in greater detail the story of how the Australian ballads developed.[3] If one poses the question, "Would Lawson and Paterson have written as they did if Gordon had never existed?" no firm answer can be given. We only know that "Gordon was the first of the literary bush-balladists."[4] We cannot be sure that his successors might not have found their way into the same literary paths, independently. We can only say that Gordon found it first.

Secondly, he made poetry, Australian poetry, popular in Australia. Regrettably, the popularity was posthumous. Like Burns, he asked for bread and was given a stone, but the presence of the stone meant more in the long run than the scarcity of bread. It meant that he had done for Australian poetry what Byron had done for Romantic poetry. He had thrust poetry before the eyes and into the consciousness, not merely of the literary public but of the literate public. His popularity could not, as it turned out, lengthen either his purse or his life, but it could provide a slightly more receptive public for Paterson, and Lawson, and later even for C. J. Dennis. Moreover, he made Australian poetry known abroad. John Galsworthy in *The Country House* makes his Mr. Paramor cite Gordon as if he had read and re-read him. Archbishop Lang, at the unveiling of the Gordon bust in 1933, claimed to "have found refreshment and exhilaration in his songs." Rudyard Kipling had read him. D. B. Wyndham Lewis and/or Charles Lee had read him (of which more anon). Even today, in spite of the incomparable literary superiority of A. D. Hope, R. D. Fitzgerald, Judith Wright, Kenneth Slessor, Douglas Stewart, and many others, it is possible that the name of Adam Lindsay Gordon is known to more people than that of any other single Australian poet. In Australia itself, it is beyond reasonable doubt that there are hundreds, if not thousands, of people who could not name a single contemporary Australian poet but who have heard of Gordon and have got pleasure from his poems.

The third influence is extra-literary; it consists of his influence, real or imputed, on the developing communal mind of the Australian nation. Douglas Sladen wished to give him all the credit for the "grim gospel of manliness" by which the typical Australian is, or was, supposed to live.[5] Though Professor Sladen was notoriously prone to exaggeration whenever any aspect of Gordon was in question, there is a grain or two of truth here. Men's lives, their attitudes and decisions, are influenced by what they have read, especially when young and especially when what they have read has made its appeal to the imagination. Therefore Adam Lindsay Gordon, immigrant and new-chum though he may have been, has a just claim to be called one of the makers of Australian culture.

CHAPTER 8

Gordon and Australia

I *The Problem*

LATE in the year 1870, a monument was set up over Gordon's grave in Brighton Cemetery. The main inscription on the face of the pedestal reads "The Poet Gordon." On May 11, 1934, his bust was unveiled in the Poet's Corner of Westminster Abbey; on its base are inscribed the words, "National Poet of Australia."

It would be an interesting study for someone to analyze in detail the steps by which Gordon came to be accepted as Australia's national poet.[1] The full story would involve literary figures like Marcus Clarke and Henry Kendall (whose memorial poem is still worth the reading), literary critics and commentators like F. W. L. Adams, A. Patchett Martin and A. G. Stephens, committee members and organizers like Major Baker and C. R. Long, and collators of information like J. K. Moir. In the center and forefront of the movement was Douglas Sladen, to whose energy and connections the Abbey bust is due.

It would seem that colonial cultures wish to have poets of their own. At least it was so in Australia, and it was certainly so in Canada. In 1880 Charles G. D. Roberts published *Orion and Other Poems*. Although his book was published by Lippincott in Philadelphia, Roberts was a Canadian, a young student living in the Maritimes and later a professor at King's College, Nova Scotia, for more than a decade. His book came into the hands of Archibald Lampman, a contemporary of Roberts and himself in later years a distinguished Canadian poet, who was then a student at Trinity College in Toronto. Lampman afterward wrote:

I sat up most of the night reading and re-reading "Orion" in a state of the wildest excitement and when I went to bed I could not sleep. It seemed to me a wonderful thing that such work could be done by a Canadian, by a young man, one of ourselves. It was like a voice from some new paradise of art, calling to us to be up and doing. . . .

I have never forgotten that morning, and its influence has always remained with me.[2]

No Australian poetry, so far as is known, ever roused quite this measure of insomniac enthusiasm, but the incident, though unusual in degree, is typical in kind. Those men in Canada and in Australia who were interested in literary activity wanted their own literature, and not to be entirely dependent on the imported article.

Before leaving this incident of Roberts and Lampman, it is worth pointing out, in view of the later controversy over Gordon's Australian qualities or lack of them, that the poem "Orion," which aroused such a pitch of nationalistic hopefulness in Lampman, is a retelling in blank verse of the classical legend of Orion the Hunter. There is nothing Canadian in it, unless we argue that the opening passage of description, which begins

> Two mighty arms of thunder-cloven rock
> Stretched ever westward toward the setting sun,
> And took into their ancient scarred embrace
> A laughing valley and a crooning bay. . . .

had a more Canadian than Grecian atmosphere.

The first fact, is that Australians wanted poets of their own, and were ready to welcome any poet who seemed to measure up to a reasonable standard as a "national poet." But why Gordon? Harpur or Kendall would seem to have had equal advantages. The primary reason was Gordon's wider popularity, which was partly due to his death and partly to the wide appeal of his later verse, especially "The Sick Stockrider" and "How We Beat the Favourite." These were read, memorized, quoted, recited, and listened to by many who had no great taste for poetry in a more formal, literary vein. And this went on, literally for generations. One finds people in Australia today, on the sunny side of middle age, who will mention that their fathers used to read Gordon's poetry to them in their early youth.

Douglas Sladen made the most of all this. "Beyond dispute," he wrote, "Gordon is the national poet of Australia. . . . And rightly, because Gordon is the voice of Australia."[3] Sladen's case is not founded on anything in Gordon's rendering of Australian landscape, or on his re-creation of the life of the Australian bush, but on the proposition that he "founded Australia's school of grim fatalism; [he] voiced Australia's code of honour."[4] His words found an echo in the judgment of many readers.

Sooner or later there would be a reaction. As *Geoffrey Hamlyn* was rejected by "Tom Collins," so Gordon came to be rejected by some as an outsider mistakenly thought to be Australian. Typical of the objectors was P. R. Stephensen, who called Gordon an *"Englishman* writing about Australia in an English way," who "never saw Australia except through his English fox-hunting squire's eyes."[5] The controversy went on, and continues to go on. The soundest and best-balanced statement is that by the late H. M. Green in the First Volume of *A History of Australian Literature,* which elaborately and convincingly argues against both extremes.

It is time to take a fresh look at the question, from a new and different point of view.

II   *The Features of Australian Culture*

The first of the controlling patterns is the familiar "clash of cultures."[6] The theme is prominent in Australian letters, and in writing about Australian letters. It appears prominently, for example, in *Back to Bool Bool,* by Brent of Bin Bin. It takes its rise from the early days of convict settlement. The convicts, representing, in a sense, no culture, regarded themselves as the people of the country, whereas the official class were mostly temporary residents whose business it was to establish English ways in the remote wilderness. By the second half of the nineteenth century the situation had changed, but the pattern remained. There were two cultures. There was the native culture as voiced by Joseph Furphy, Henry Lawson, and Steele Rudd; and there was "culture" as found in the cities and on the larger stations, where English books were read, English music played, and English manners and customs kept up.

This split is not exclusively Australian. In Canada before World War I, and even to some extent in the 1920's and 1930's, the same divisions could be found. There were farmhouses, and working-class houses, where there were few or no books, where conversation was generally limited to local gossip, where there was a lively contempt of anything "English," and where the favorite form of musical entertainment was a small supply of phonograph records by Harry Lauder. (Lauder, being Scotch, hardly counted as a foreigner.) Those who lived in such houses might be Presbyterians or Methodists, but very seldom Anglicans. There were other houses, mostly in town but sometimes on the farms, where one felt the influence of colonial gentility surviving, and where

there were plenty of English books, both popular and classic.
Gordon's place in all this is indecisive. In his poetry there is
no sense of the clash of cultures, because there is a co-existence
of cultures. The Australian side is in the low-brow jocularity of
"Hippodromania," in much of "Ye Wearie Wayfarer," muted in
"From the Wreck," and of course in full cry in "The Sick Stockrider." It is also present in "How We Beat the Favourite," in
spite of its English locale. But nearly all the rest is from the outside, including "Podas Okus," "The Romance of Britomarte," and
the bulk of what lies between.

One could ask, in the vernacular, so what? No one has complained that Browning is un-English because his epic is set in
Italy. In fact, Browning's "English" poems make a smaller proportion to the whole, quantitatively (and a still smaller proportion qualitatively), than do Gordon's Australian poems. In fact,
the controversy over Gordon's Australian-ness is itself a part, and
a symbol, of the clash of cultures.

The lines from Fytte VIII of "Ye Wearie Wayfarer" are
symbolic:

> Hark! the bells on distant cattle
> Waft across the range,
> Through the golden-tufted wattle,
> Music low and strange;
> Like the marriage peal of fairies
> Comes the tinkling sound,
> Or like chimes of sweet St. Mary's
> On far English ground.

Here the two landscapes are set side by side. But the Australian
reader would feel that the English side has the strong, nostalgic
appeal, whereas the Australian is feebler and incidental. Gordon
was aware of the two cultures; he put them both into his poetry,
but he did not quite succeed in fusing them.

The concept of "mateship" is fundamental among Australian
attitudes, and nowhere in literature stronger than in the stories
of Henry Lawson. It was a natural outgrowth of the conditions
of life in the bush and on the diggings. A man depended on his
mate for companionship and for assistance, and in emergencies
for his life. In literature the concept is comparable to that of the
posse comitatus in Greek and Germanic epic, with the difference
that it was the pair, not the group, which counted most.

The concept was weak in Gordon, for two reasons. One was
that it had not yet appeared in literature with the emphasis

which Lawson was to give it, and Gordon was not the man to
make that innovation. He was by nature a good deal of a lone
wolf. He had mates; what man has not? There was Charley
Walker in England, and there was Harry Stockdale, and William
Trainor in Australia—possibly also Edward Bright, who is said
to have been the original of the sick stockrider. But he was not
a man to "make a thing of" mateship. Moreover, he could only
succeed in conveying the flavor of mateship in the Australian
poems. This he does, and does well, in "The Sick Stockrider."
Ned and the stockrider have been together for many years and
have been through work, adventure, and play together. More
important, Ned is playing the typical mate's part, as the opening
lines of the poem emphasize. He is conveying his sick mate to a
place of rest and help. There are traces of mateship in "From
the Wreck," and in "Wolf and Hound," but such faint traces that
they would not be noticed if one were not looking for them. And
in "The Rhyme of Joyous Garde," though the relationship between Arthur and Lancelot is portrayed from the beginning as
one very like that of mateship, in spite of the difference in rank,
the scene is so far from Australia that it does not count. The
same thing is true of the relationship between Laurence and
Forrest, in "Ten Paces Off." The sum of the matter is that Gordon
had the ideal of mateship in his poetry, but he did not proclaim
it clearly enough, emphatically enough, or often enough to be
counted to him for nationalistic righteousness.

A third element was a somber realism, and what Professor
Moore has called "the shadow of drought." In Gordon's day Australia was a difficult country in which to make a living, and in
some parts it still is. Some men became rich, professional men
in the cities, successful merchants, and fortunate station-owners.
But the predominant impression in literature was one of poverty
and insecurity. Indeed, to be settled and well-off seems a little
un-Australian.

This feature of Australian literature persists to this day, and
it is paradoxical. Australia is a highly urbanized nation, and very
much of a middle-class society. Yet the Australian novel, with a
few exceptions, sticks stubbornly to the portrayal of the rural
proletariat or of the urban proletariat. Patrick White, probably
the best known of Australian novelists today, does both, in *The
Tree of Man* and *Riders in the Chariot* respectively. In the first,
we are made to feel strongly that the middle-class, well-to-do
characters are alien, distant, and irrelevant.

Behind this mood is the nature of the land. Once outside the cities, and the fertile parts of eastern and southern Australia, the country is dark, lonely, and arid. At Broken Hill, N.S.W., a still prosperous mining town in the midst of the desert, there is a golf course, but it has no true putting greens. It has, instead, surfaces of fine slag from the mines, which the player is allowed by local rules to scrape smooth in the line of his putt before making the shot. And even the fertile farming areas of New South Wales and Victoria are lonely, to an American eye—unless, of course, the American comes from Texas.

Gordon does not fail to render this aspect of Australia. The feel of it is in "Wolf and Hound," and there is a touch of it in "A Song of Autumn," in the reference to "the burnt-up banks [that] are yellow and sad, / When the boughs are yellow and sere." The best expression is in "De Te," the poem about the finding of a suicide's body in open country within the sight of the sea.

> We heard the hound beneath the mound,
>   We scared the swamp hawk hovering nigh—
> We had not sought for that we found—
>   He lay as dead men only lie.

This almost takes us into the world of Barcroft Boake.

He does not so well render the complementary feeling of the spell of the lonely country, which is also one of the elements in the Australian pattern of attitudes. "Tom Collins," we feel, despite his somewhat troublesome wanderings, would not really have chosen to live anywhere else. Gordon responded to that fascination in his life, but not much in his poetry. His portrayal of the outdoor life is somber; he does not quite give us its appeal.

It has to be admitted that Gordon did not really feel the spell of the bush. His choice was for the outdoors, but his was the outdoors of "God's glorious oxygen," not the outdoors of God's arid sand or mallee scrub. His chosen work was with horses; and horses, trained horses, belong to civilization. His chosen sport was racing, and races, however far from town the course may be located, is essentially a gentlemanly or a suburban activity, or both. When he does write of the bush, his attention is not on the bush but on what it contains and serves as a setting for. In "De Te" it is on the suicide's body; in "The Sick Stockrider" it is on the activities and adventures which he and his mate had enjoyed. Only in "A Dedication" does he describe with his eye, and his ear, on the object.

Another quality absent from Gordon's writing is the sense of the vigor of earth, and of men close to the earth. Or rather, it is almost absent, because we have to reckon once again with "The Sick Stockrider."

> 'Twas merry in the glowing morn, among the gleaming grass,
>   To wander as we've wander'd many a mile,
> And blow the cool tobacco cloud, and watch the white
>   wreaths pass,
>   Sitting loosely in the saddle all the while;
> 'Twas merry 'mid the blackwoods when we spied the station
>   roofs,
>   To wheel the wild scrub cattle at the yard,
> With a running fire of stockwhips and a fiery run of hoof,
>   Oh! the hardest day was never then too hard!

Here we feel the strength of liveliness that comes to men because they live close to the earth. It is more vigorous than the corresponding feeling we get from Henry Lawson or Joseph Furphy. When we get this scene from Lawson, it is the sense of stubbornness, and sometimes of sullenness, that we feel, not the *élan* that Gordon expresses. A couple of generations later, Patrick White was to make much more of this theme of the stubborn strength of the man of the earth, in *The Tree of Man*. Gordon made little of it.

It might be argued that he rationalizes the theme in the lines from "Cui Bono":

> By sea or by soil man is bound to toil,
>   And the dreamer, waiting for time and tide,
> For awhile may shirk his share of the work,
>   But he grows with his dream dissatisfied.

The contrast between the toiler and the dreamer is much to Australian taste, as it would have been to Canadian taste in the same period, but it is not part of the pattern we have been looking for.

The remaining elements of the pattern are social rather than natural, and, like the clash of cultures, concern what men thought and said more than their feelings about nature. The first of these is the "radical democracy" which was strongly enunciated by Furphy and which persists to this day. In 1897 Furphy announced to A. G. Stephens and ultimately to the world that his new novel was democratic in temper and offensively Australian in bias.[7] The two were largely identical; the Australian bias was radically democratic.

One reason for this is not hard to find. It arose out of one aspect of the "clash of cultures" already mentioned. Here again the comparison with conditions in Canada is instructive. In Canada of the 1830's, for example, immigrants from England who came with an exaggerated sense of their own gentility were quickly disillusioned, partly owing to the nearness of the great American democracy and the influx of "Yankee" immigrants in the early years of the century.[8] Purely social distinctions were worn down, and where they persisted were exceptions rather than the rule. There were great differences in wealth and education, but little inherited social status, as such. The crossing-sweeper did not ordinarily dine with the bank manager, but if he did he would come in by the front door and be treated like anyone else. In Australia the hierarchical structure of society was more widely maintained. "Social status," wrote Furphy, "apart from all consideration of mind, manners, or even money, is more accurately weighed on a right-thinking Australian station than anywhere else in the world."[9] Now, a social or political idea, like an electrical charge, tends to induce its opposite. As a result, democracy was a more radical sentiment in Australia than in Canada because, while in Canada the social stratification, being inappropriate to the country, dropped out of sight in most places, in Australia it was maintained, although even more inappropriate.[10]

In this matter Australia retains a curious ambivalence in relation to the rest of the English-speaking world. It retains side by side the democratic attitudes shared by the Americans and the sense of social hierarchy derived from the Old World. It combines the radical democracy of its public manners, its political parties, its powerful labor unions, and its buses and bathing beaches, with the survival of aristocratic, or *hautbourgeois* tone of the more conservative institutions of education and government. In the armed services, we are told, the organization is necessarily hierarchical but the tone is democratic.

Gordon's place in this is peculiar. He was on both sides, being an aristocrat by nature but associating from choice with the ordinary people of his community. The poetry is in the aristocratic tradition. It is the poetry of feudal daring and feudal obligation, with the dash of D'Artagnan and the code of cavaliers. His characters are in the tradition of the English public school man of 1914 who "had been taught that it was the mark of a gentleman to welcome danger, and to regard the risk of death as the most piquant sauce to life."[11] The figure of Nolan at Balclava is a distillation of this tradition. Gordon's democracy consisted in the

assumption that this tradition was not necessarily the preroga-
tive of a class and that manliness was not limited to gentlemen.
He did not care about votes, nor about equalized wealth. We do
not know that he objected to the hierarchical snobbery of the
stations, although he took care that he himself would not be sent
off to the "men's hut." He was desirous of being recognized as a
"gentleman," and was to that extent undemocratic. On the other
hand, he gives to his policemen and to his stockrider the courage
and dash that belonged to the gentleman of tradition, and to
that extent may be called egalitarian. This is not the radical
democracy of the political reformer, but it may be more genu-
inely radical than theirs.

He had, however, none of the utopianism of the Great Australian Dream, whatever form that may be understood to take.
One form goes back to the days of W. C. Wentworth:

> May this, thy last-born infant, then arise,
> To glad thy heart and greet thy parent eyes;
> And Australasia float, with flag unfurl'd,
> A new Britannia in another world.[12]

This version of an Australian dream is, so to speak, two-edged.
It suggests a glorious future, but not the kind of future that later
generations believed in. The "new Britannia" calls up images of
imitation, and of a transplanted culture quite different from the
world of "The Banjo" or the "Sentimental Bloke." Gordon was
mainly indifferent to both potentialities. The idea, if anyone had
it, of an antipodal Britain, complete with country houses, crum-
pets and tea, and "going to the office in the train," did not move
him, and neither did the prospect of general prosperity for all,
in a land of new, indigenous culture.

The principal causes are simple, and two in number. The first
is that Gordon as a poet looked more to the past than did any
other poet of his time and place. His materials came, in large
measure, from the romantic past of King Arthur and King
Charles; from the "Gothic" past in *Ashtaroth;* or from the equally
romantic, anachronistic, life-in-death present of Lord Cardigan
and Lord Raglan. Though we have treated him as a Victorian
(and he was one), we need shift the angle of vision by only a
few degrees in order to see him as a Romantic born out of due
time.[13]

The second reason is that Gordon's gloomy, realistic, Celtic
temperament forbade him to entertain utopian visions of a future
great society. He did not believe in "a good time coming." He

knew that there is always a "bad time coming," however satisfying the present may be. "The troubles of life are many, / The
pleasures of life are few;" he wrote in "Wormwood and Nightshade." As an agnostic (and it is hard to see how we can regard
him as anything else) he had no sustaining hope of "pie in the
sky, by and by, when you die," but he was grimly conscious of
the prospects of gruel on the earth before you die, unless you
are lucky enough to die early and glamorously like Nolan. He
was able to accept the *status quo,* not because he was satisfied
with it, but because the human lot, on balance, does not improve
very much. Even if we could effectively curb man's inhumanity
to man (and taking the world over we are not making much
progress in that direction) we would still find, for example, that
by reducing infant mortality we have increased the sum of pain
from malnutrition, cancer, and coronary heart disease. Gordon
was no utopian. Any hopes he may have had for the great future
of Australia find no echo in his poetry.

The other side to the utopian temper was the satirical, and the
humorous. Australian verse is in this matter contrasted with
Canadian. The Canadian poets took themselves and their voca-
tion seriously, and apart from "The Cremation of Sam McGee"
there is little humor in Canadian verse. In Australia, on the other
hand, *The Songs of a Sentimental Bloke* sold in their thousands,
appealing as they did both to the democratic taste and to the
sense of humor in their Australian audience. C. J. Dennis was
fundamentally humorous, and Robert W. Service only occasionally so.

Gordon was no humorist. During his career as a member of
parliament, he is said to have spent much of his time in the
house making caricatures of fellow members, so that a frequent
greeting among the legislators was, "Have you seen Gordon's
latest?"[14] But his poetry was, as the schoolboy said about Matthew Arnold, "no place to go for a laugh," although one might
get a quiet smile from part of Fytte IV of "Ye Weàrie Wayfarer."

Next is the notorious "humanism" of Australia. This is humanism in the modern sense, not that of the days of Erasmus. Robert
Sherrod, writing for an American popular magazine in the early
1950's, before the Olympic Games were held at Melbourne, testified that "Several ex-servicemen mentioned . . . that the most
striking thing about Australians was their total lack of interest in
religion."[15] This may be an exaggeration. Australia is well supplied with churches. Nor are these churches empty. But they are
fewer and smaller than in England, in relation to the population.
What is more, the tone of Australian life, and certainly the tone

of Australian literature, is humanist. Religion plays an even
smaller part in the novels of Australia than in the novels of Jane
Austen.

Gordon the man was part of this climate of opinion. In spite
of his long and grateful friendship with Father Woods, he had
no habits of worship, no sense for the supernatural, and certainly
no dependence on the providence or protection of any super-
human power. He .was not, so far as we can judge, anti-clerical.
Harry Stockdale, in his published reminiscences,[16] avers that
Gordon "wanted formal religion left out of the schools altogther,"
but we cannot build much on that. Clergymen have sometimes
said the same thing. He was simply an agnostic, a more serious
agnostic than "Tom Collins," a thinking man who had thought
about the meaning of life and death and had come to no conclusion except that man is up against the ineluctable unknown.

Gordon the poet was a slightly different matter. More than
other Australian writers he deals in images of life after death, of
a "Maker" to whom the souls may "fly" (as in "Unshriven"), and
of a final assize when "the souls shall be summon'd from land
and sea, / At the blast of His bright archangel" ("The Rhyme of
Joyous Garde"). The main reason for this is that these are poems
of the past, of an age of faith, and such images belong naturally
to them. They are dramatic; they reflect little, and may reflect
nothing, of the mind of the poet.[17]

There is one poem which is different. It is not clearly either of
the present or the past, and it expresses this theme with unusual
directness. It is "From Lightning and Tempest," printed in *Sea
Spray and Smoke Drift.* There are two stanzas. In the first, the
spring-wind blows through the forest, the cedars wave their
branches, the oaks stand firm, and the men sing:

> "Let us follow our own devices, and foster our own desires.
> As firm as our oaks in our pride, as our cedars fair in our
>   sight,
>   We stand like the trees of the forest that brave the frosts
>   and the fires."

Then the storm comes to the forest, and the plague to the town,
and the men are found

> Crying—"God; we have sinn'd, we have sinn'd,
> We are bruised, we are shorn, we are thinn'd,
>   Our strength is turn'd to derision, our pride laid low
>   in the dust.

Our cedars are cleft by Thy lightnings, our oaks are strewed
  by Thy wind,
And we fall on our faces seeking Thine aid, though Thy
  wrath is just."

This is the negation of humanism, or the failure of humanism, or,
more bluntly, the failure of nerve which is the nemesis of humanism. It is uncharacteristic of the Australian spirit, at least in literature. That spirit takes whatever comes, without appealing to
heaven for an unearned increment of supernatural deliverance.

On one final count Gordon is even more positively un-Australian. The bushranger became the hero of Australian legend and
ballad through the nineteenth century. The legend persists, soft-
ened and hallowed by time, into the middle of the twentieth
century, when Glenrowan, where the Kellys made their last stand
against the police, has acquired something of the aura of a national shrine and where the relics of Ned Kelly's career are preserved and periodically displayed for the veneration of the
faithful.[18] The feeling is reasonable. Few of the early inhabitants
of Australia had reason to love the law. Their sympathies were
inevitably on the side of the outlaw. Also, it would seem that
those who stood for law and order—the bureaucracy and the
police—were a good deal this side of perfection in their sense of
fairness or humanity. Whether this was the result of a system
that warped the souls both of those who suffered under it and of
those who administered it, as is suggested by Price Warung in
"John Price's Bar of Steel,"[19] is not important. Even the fact of
the matter is not important. Whether the policemen, prison offi-
cials, and magistrates were unjust and vindictive or not, there
was a popular impression to that effect. The bushranger was
therefore a man as much sinned against as sinning, and with the
added glamor of nonconformity and daring.

Twice does the bushranger enter Gordon's verse. The first occasion is in "The Sick Stockrider," in which the speaker in his
memories recalls a lively brush that he and Ned had had in the
old days.

Ay! we had a glorious gallop after "Starlight" and his gang,
  When they bolted from Sylvester's on the flat;
How the sun-dried reed-beds crackled, how the flint-strewn
    ranges rang
  To the strokes of "Mountaineer" and "Acrobat";
. . . .
We led the hunt throughout, Ned, on the chestnut and the
  grey,

> And the troopers were three hundred yards behind,
>   While we emptied our six-shooters on the bushrangers at bay,
>   In the creek with stunted box-tree for a blind!

The other instance is "Wolf and Hound," in which the hero is the
policeman, who bravely follows the outlaw into the cave and
gives him the death which we are led to feel was well deserved.
On this point Gordon must be admitted to be against the pre-
vailing mood of his adopted culture. Not only so, but his attitude
is positively English, which makes matters worse. He does indeed see this feature of Australia through an "English fox-hunting squire's eyes."[20] His inheritance was aristocratic, and though
not above mad escapades it was fundamentally on the side of
the law. His father was an army officer and a schoolmaster; both
professions inculcate sympathy with those who preserve discipline and enmity toward those who break it. Besides, Gordon had
a strong association between the image of bravery and the glamor
of uniformed discipline. "The Roll of the Kettledrum" begins:

> One line of swart profiles, and bearded lips dressing,
>   One ridge of bright helmets, one crest of fair plumes,
> One streak of blue sword-blades all bared for the fleshing,
>   One row of red nostrils that scent battle-fumes.

Standing first in his gallery of heroes (Burke being the second)
was Nolan, the young cavalry officer who was killed in the
Charge of the Light Brigade. Harry Stockdale's evidence on this
point is probably reliable. His "pencilled notes," preserved in the
Mitchell Library, testify to Gordon's intensely emotional admiration of Nolan, and identify him as the young officer killed in the
charge at Balaclava. Gordon's own comment in verse is in the
fifth stanza of "Part I.—Visions in the Smoke," in "Hippodromania":

> Where bullets whistle, and round shot whiz,
>   Hoofs trample, and blades flash bare,
> God send me an ending fair as his
>   Who died in his stirrups there!

Such images being in the background of his mind, it is not surprising that he gave his admiration, not to the bushranger or the
outlaw, but to the Police Trooper who risked life, and perhaps
reputation as well, to capture him.
      There is one more possibility. Gordon was by nature a good

deal of a nonconformist. He may well have sided with the police partly because the public opinion of his world was with the outlaws. But this was at most a minor motive. It is significant that when Gordon was asked to stand for parliament, his backers were from the Squatters' Party,[21] and that after his election he spoke, though not very effectively, in favor of the squatters' interests.

So far we have been dealing with the content of Gordon's verse, and the attitudes to be found there, in relation to the characteristically Australian attitudes as they can be detected in literature. There is also the question of style, mainly of diction, which is pertinent here. How far does Gordon's choice of words make him an Australian writer?

Comparisons are important. Is there an Australian diction? Certainly there are words which suggest an Australian setting, and Gordon used some of them in "A Dedication": "wattle," for example, and "trunks Eucalyptian." Yet it is self-evident that it takes more than an occasional reference to wattle or gum-trees, or, as in "The Sick Stockrider," to "stockwhips" or "tea-tree scrub" to give a poem an Australian flavor with any body to it. Consider what Henry Lawson does at the opening of "The Teams":

> A cloud of dust on the long, white road,
>   And the teams go creeping on
> Inch by inch with the weary load;
> And by the power of the green-hide goad
>   The distant goal is won.

There is no single word here, except "green-hide," that Gordon might not have used in any of his poems. But if we consider the diction, not word by word, but in its texture, and in relation to the picture it creates, the effect is Australian beyond anything that Gordon gives us.

It may be objected that Lawson came a full generation later than Gordon, by which time the sense of what was peculiarly Australian had had opportunity to develop. But Henry Kendall was Gordon's contemporary, and Kendall was able to write:

> The wallaroos grope through the tufts of the grass,
> And turn to their coverts for fear;
> But he sits in the ashes and lets them pass
> Where the boomerangs sleep with the spear—
> With the nullah, the sling, and the spear.

> ("The Last of His Tribe")

There is more to this stanza than the references to wallaroos and boomerangs; there is a sense of weight in the scene, which is an Australian mood, and different in its effect from what we find, as a general rule, in Gordon's verse.

On the other hand, Kendall did not always write in this vein, and Gordon sometimes did. If we look, for example, at the seventh stanza of Kendall's "Orara,"

> The singing silver life I hear,
>   Whose home is in the green
> Far-folded woods of fountains clear,
>   Where I have never been,

we are nearer to A. E. Housman than we are to C. J. Dennis or Will Ogilvie. Then if we turn to the third section of "Wolf and Hound" we find:

> I turned away with no fixed intent
>   And headed for Hawthorndell;
> I could neither eat in the splitter's tent
>   Nor drink at the splitter's well;
> I knew that they gloried in my mishap,
>   And I cursed them between my teeth—
> A blood-red sunset through Brayton's Gap
>   Flung a lurid fire on the heath.

In diction we have one common noun and two place-names which may be taken to suggest the Australian scene, though splitters are to be found elsewhere in the world. In this context, the clause "they gloried in my mishap" represents an Australian state of mind. But the final line works in the opposite direction; to the American reader, at least, it has an English rather than Australian air, largely because of the established connotations of the word "heath."

The most that we can assert is that Gordon's vocabulary seldom reflects his Australian environment, nor does the imagery which he constructs with it. In this he shows a marked difference from the later writers such as Henry Lawson, and he falls short of Kendall—though not, one feels, by much. To demonstrate this fully would require a complicated exercise in statistical criticism.

III   *Gordon's Position*

What constitutes an Australian writer, or a Canadian writer, or an American writer? This question has never been satisfactorily answered. About most writers, of course, there is no doubt. Miles Franklin is certainly Australian, as Archibald Lampman was Canadian and William Faulkner, American. It is the borderline case that makes the difficulty, and makes us search for an agreed basis of classification which is really not to be found.

Is the birthplace of a writer decisive? If it were, Gordon would be neither an English nor an Australian writer, but Azorean. But it is not, not quite. No one ever thinks of Stephen Leacock as anything but a Canadian writer although he was born in England. A lively nationalism may try to claim Havelock Ellis and Professor Gilbert Murray for the Antipodes, but the world at large is not inclined to concede the claim.[22]

The place of education is a more important criterion. There are two awkward precedents here, in the persons of Henry James and T. S. Eliot. Eliot was born in Missouri and educated at Harvard, and later at Oxford and the Sorbonne; he not only spent the whole of his working life in England but became a veritable *Anglus Anglorum*. James began his writing career in America, and used American characters and American themes in his books, but the major part of his education was European and he lived more than half his life as an Englishman in England. In spite of which, both James and Eliot are customarily represented in the large-scale anthologies of American literature[23] and in libraries their books are shelved with American rather than English literature. To follow these precedents would mean classifying Gordon as English, not Australian. There are, however, other precedents. No one disputes Joseph Conrad's place in English literature, though he was a man full grown before he began to use the English language; and Charles Heavysege retains his place in Canadian poetry (such as it is) though he came to Canada at the age of thirty-six.

The third consideration is the place of residence during the bulk of a writer's adult years, and especially the most productive years. Seldom does this count for much. James and Eliot have been mentioned. Henry Handel Richardson remains an Australian writer though she went to Europe before she was out of her teens and never returned except as a visitor. Canadian examples vary. One one side there is Bliss Carman, always regarded in Canada as one of the foremost Canadian poets of his period in spite of his years of residence in the United States. On the other, there is Thomas B. Costain, who was born in Canada and who worked as a journalist in Canada until he was thirty-five, but who is generally thought of as an American writer and who is desribed in the Index to the *Encyclopaedia Americana* (Canadian Edition, 1963) as "Amer. ed., au."

The fourth question is that of an author's material and attitudes, what he writes about and how he writes about it. It established bodies of literature the question does not arise; in "colonial" literatures, it does. Shakespeare would still be an English poet-playwright though he had never written the chronicle plays, but if Henry Handel Richardson had never written *The Fortunes of Richard Mahony*—and if she had written several novels like *Maurice Guest*—she would hardly stand today in the ranks of Australian novelists. Outside Australasia, except for serious students, not many readers think of Katherine Mansfield or Ngaio Marsh as New Zealand writers; while Stuart Cloete is thought of as a South African novelist although he was born in France, was educated in France and England, served with the British Army, settled in South Africa when he was nearly thirty, and published his first novel of South African life when he was forty. The difference lies partly in the places of residence of these writers, but even more in the things they wrote about. "The Garden Party," in spite of the use of the word "mate," suggests an English or American setting. Miss Marsh's Superintendent Alleyn belongs to London. As for Stuart Cloete, even his titles (*Turning Wheels*, 1937; *The Curve and the Tusk*, 1953) can be redolent of their African setting.

In relation to what has been said, Gordon's place in Australian literature is made to seem uncertain. He was not born in Australia. He was not educated in Australia. Even though he spent the whole of his working life in Australia, he presents only some, and by no means all, of the themes and social patterns characteristic of Australian literature. Compared with that of Lawson, or Paterson, or O'Dowd, or even Kendall, his verse has little to offer which is markedly Australian.

The fact is that there is no agreed principle on which the classification can be made.[24] There is one simplified solution to be suggested. Ask these three questions about any writer: where was he born and educated? where did he mainly live during his productive life? what did he mainly write about, and what themes and patterns of life did he portray? Then, if any two of the three questions lead to the same answer, let that be the answer to the question as to where he rightly belongs. So the argument might run. It is revealing, and troublesome, to find that even this simplification does not wholly solve the problem. Mechanically applied, it could exclude Byron and Browning from the ranks of English poets. It would leave Henry Handel Richardson as an Australian novelist, since *The Fortunes of Richard Mahony* is a larger-scale work, and probably better known, than *Maurice Guest,* but it would still leave Adam Lindsay Gordon teetering on the verge. Why, then, is Gordon to be called an Australian poet? Here we come, at last, to the nub of the matter. When all the arguments on both sides have been exhausted, there remain two decisive factors. The first is that no one else wanted him. The second is that the Australians themselves did, and accepted him with widespread and continuing enthusiasm.

The first of these statements is not so disparaging as it sounds. It is connected with a further consideration deliberately omitted from the previous analysis; namely, the place of publication. This factor works in one direction only and is not reversible. If an author is on all other counts indisputably Australian or Canadian, he becomes no less so by having his books published in England or in the U.S.A. Both Charles G. D. Roberts and Bliss Carman had their early volumes published in the United States. But if an author has his books published in Australia or Canada, and not until much later, if at all, in one of the metropolitan centers of the English-speaking world, he is more likely to be accepted as an Australian or Canadian author. Gordon's poems had their early publication in Australia, and by the time they reached any English publication that acceptance had been firmly established.[25]

If Gordon's poems had been published first in London instead of Melbourne, what would their fate have been? They could hardly have been more completely ignored than they actually were in the years 1867 to 1870. Would an English public have paid more attention to them? Probably not, for various reasons. It was not that Gordon's poetry was necessarily inferior to much that had been temporarily well received, but that it lacked what someone has called "quantity of quality," and would almost certainly have been lost among the quantities of verse appearing at the time. The closing years of his final decade saw the publication of *The Life and Death of Jason* and of *The Earthly Paradise,* to give but one example. Among the great number of poems, long and short, coming to the attention of the English reading public, Gordon's conventional lays and romances would have proved too light for the counterpoise of so great an opposition. His unconventional pieces, those that gave him his first hold on Australian readers, would have less appeal to English tastes.

The decisive fact is that the Australian public, from 1870, accepted Gordon as one of their own poets, and as their favorite poet. Douglas Sladen asserted that "nearly every family" in Victoria and South Australia owned Gordon's poems, and that they were "better known than any English poet's are known in England."[26] The Reverent J. J. Malone is more convincing, because he is more modest in his attitude and more circumstantial in his testimony. About ten years before Sladen, he wrote in a pamphlet on Gordon published, rather oddly, by the Australian Catholic Truth Society:

The most a man can do legitimately is to register his own experience, and the experience which I have gathered from the authorities in the Public Library, and from the leading booksellers in the city, from the friends with whom I have come in contact, from the various societies with which I have been familiar, and the many entertainments of all kinds at which I have been present, is that Adam Lindsay Gordon is far and away the most popular of all the poets of our island continent.[27]

There is also extant a letter written by A. G. Stephens from the publishing firm of A. H. Massina & Co., on January 3, 1903, which provides authoritative statistical evidence of the pre-eminence in sales (and presumably in readership) of Gordon's books.[28]

A few years ago, one of Canada's leading authorities on Victorian poetry was asked, during the course of a discussion: "Who decided that Tennyson and Browning are major poets?" The answer came in one word, "Posterity." Similarly, to the question, "Who decided that Adam Lindsay Gordon is an Australian poet?" the answer is, "The Australians." F. W. L. Adams in 1893 referred to Gordon as "the inspired spokesman of the actual effects of the Australian climate and manner of living."[29] As recently as 1949, D. H. Rankin, in a book on *The Development and Philosophy of Australian Aestheticism*, described the typical Australian as one who "follows the teaching of the poet, Adam Lindsay Gordon, who taught the sportsman's creed: fearlessness, comradeship, adventure, and the love for the open-air life."[30]

It has to be admitted that Gordon's position as an Australian poet has been due in no small degree to cultural lobbying, through Gordon societies, memorial plaques and statues, pilgrimages, and other manifestations of the "Gordonian Movement." When we have allowed for all that, when we have given full weight to the dissenting opinions expressed by Stephensen and others, when we have recognized that Gordon expressed little of the Australian landscape and by no means all the Australian attitudes, when we have examined his vocabulary and found it scanty in Australian coinages, when we have seen him as an imperfectly naturalized immigrant, the conclusion stands, that

> In spite of all temptations
> To belong to other nations,
> He remains Australian!

CHAPTER 9

Postlude

THERE is an anecdote of a tightrope performer who at the climax of his performance stood on his head at the middle of the tightrope and in that inverted posture played on a violin. On one occasion a critical spectator, after listening for a few bars, remarked to his companion, "Heifetz he ain't." The parallel is inexact, although Gordon did in a metaphorical sense stand on his head at certain junctures of his life. Indeed, when we consider his reported modes of composing his poetry on horseback or sprawling in the crook of a gum-tree, we might argue that he did so in a quasi-literal sense as well. However, the anecdote is introduced, not for the performer, but for the hypercritical spectator. There are innumerable violinists worth listening to who are not Heifetz, nor Oistrakh, nor Menuhin.

There is simply not quite enough bad poetry being written today. This is not a paradox. It is a sober statement of a plain truth. As a general rule, any human activity reaches superlative excellence only where it is being widely practiced by a great many people. That means that it is being done badly. The Sam Sneads and Arnold Palmers come from a culture in which there are thousands of golfers who brag for a month if they break a hundred. The best cricketers come from regions where village cricket is continually played, matches in which a score of thirty gives a batsman an enviable reputation. It is an obvious geometrical fact that the higher a pyramid goes the broader must be its base.

In the pyramidal structure of poetic quality, at any given time, poetry like Gordon's does not belong at, or even near, the apex, *pace* Professor Sladen. Neither does it belong near the base among the poetasters or weekend producers of doggerel. It belongs rather somewhere in the middle of the muse's favors. For all that, it has a rightful place, and it is not only important, it is indispensable that that place should be occupied. Once it is believed that poetry is to be written only by geniuses capable of immortal verse, the supply of geniuses is likely to grow strangely thin.

142

Two factors have greatly hindered a just appreciation of Gordon's poetry. The first is the one we have been hinting at, the notion that unless poetry is "great" it is not worth reading. It is analogous to the "hit-theory" that is eroding the theatrical life of the older metropolitan centers today. It is not true. There are many readers who have got from Gordon the pleasure proper to poetry, but whom Milton or Yeats would leave cold. What is more, even the experienced reader needs poetry on many levels of quality. No one really knows Shakespeare until he has learned to read with some appreciation the plays of Shakespeare's lesser contemporaries, Kyd, Marlowe, Webster, Tourneur. What do they know of poetry who know only Milton and Wordsworth and T. S. Eliot? Not enough.

The second difficulty is the irrelevant but persistent habit of nationalistic criticism. Some have extravagantly overpraised him because he was Australian; other have pointlessly decried him because, in their view, he was not Australian. Few, until recently, have displayed anything like the balanced objectivity that Francis W. L. Adams had achieved by 1890. There are signs that such a balanced view is now becoming more widely possible.[1] As it spreads, Gordon will be appreciated, if not more widely at least more judiciously.

There are two oddly interesting facts to be set down in this penultimate position. In 1930, D. B. Wyndham Lewis and Charles Lee collected a bookful of miscellaneous verses which they published under the title *The Stuffed Owl, An Anthology of Bad Verse*. In that volume Adam Lindsay Gordon occupies three pages, inclusive of a brief headnote, chiefly biographical, in which there are only three trivial errors in seven lines. Anyone who thinks this a very left-handed compliment, which discretion would overlook, is advised to read the Preface to *The Stuffed Owl*, and also to ponder on the fact that Gordon is here placed in the company of Dryden, Crabbe, Byron, Wordsworth, Keats, and Tennyson. Moreover, when Kipling wrote the set of parodies which appear in the Definitive Edition under the general title, "The Muse Among the Motors," Gordon was one of the poets he chose to parody. In so doing, he ranged Gordon alongside Horace, Chaucer, Milton, Wordsworth, and Shakespeare, to name but a few. A poet worth parodying is usually worth reading.

The final point to be urged is that Gordon is worth reading, not because he is a great poet nor because he is an Australian poet, but simply because he is a poet. "Milton he ain't." Perhaps he has more of the defects of his qualities than the qualities of his defects. That does not greatly matter. Let him be read for whatever each reader may find that he has to offer, without undue attention to the captious cavilings of querulous critics, nationalistic or academic. Let him have a fair field and no artificial disfavor. A spokesman all his life, he would ask no more.

Notes and References

Chapter One

1. Edith Humphris, *The Life of Adam Lindsay Gordon* (London, n.d.), pp. 48, 53.
2. Letter in the Mitchell Library, Sydney, N.S.W.
3. Holograph letter in the Mitchell Library.
4. Letter in the South Australian Archives, Adelaide, S.A.
5. Cf. Patrick White, *The Tree of Man* (London, 1956), Chap. 18.
6. J. Howlett Ross, *A Memoir of the Life of Adam Lindsay Gordon* (London, 1892), pp. 39-41.
7. Douglas Sladen, *Adam Lindsay Gordon,* the "Westminster Abbey Memorial Volume" (London, n.d.), pp. 76 f.
8. Letter to Riddoch, in F. M. Robb (ed.), *The Poems of Adam Lindsay Gordon* (Melbourne, 1962), p. 370.
9. Mr. and Mrs. T. H. Ilbury, in *Western Australian Historical Society Journal and Proceedings,* Vol. I, Part 2 (1928), pp. 56-60.
10. Robb., *op. cit.,* p. liv.
11. *Ibid.,* p. lxv.
12. For the date, see Robb, pp. 361 f. Moir places it later.
13. Adelaide *Advertiser,* March 23, 1912, pp. 19 f. See also Edith Humphris and Douglas Sladen, *Adam Lindsay Gordon and His Friends in England and Australia* (London, 1912), pp. 79-90, *passim.*
14. T. S. Eliot, *On Poetry and Poets* (London, 1957), p. 98.
15. See above, p. 15.
16. See *Southerly,* V, i, 26-28.
17. Rev. J. J. Malone, *Gordon: The Australian Poet* (Melbourne, n.d., but cat. 1904). See pp. 9 ff.
18. Francis W. L. Adams, *Australian Essays* (Melbourne and London, 1886), p. 20.
19. *The Feud* was reprinted in 1964, with notes by Hugh Anderson, in a thirty-six-page volume issued by Rigby, at Adelaide.
20. The copyright was later transferred to Clarson, Massina & Co. For many years the accepted order of publication placed *Sea Spray and Smoke Drift* first.

Chapter Two

1. Wordsworth's *Preface* of 1800, *passim*, and T. S. Eliot, *On Poetry and Poets* (London, 1957) p. 18.
2. The lines are quoted in Ernest Raymond's *Tell England* (Book I, Chapter III), a popular novel of World War I, of which there were more than thirty printings. They also appear in John Galworthy's *The Country House*, Chapter IX.
3. Guy Butler (ed.), *A Book of South African Verse* (London, 1959).

Chapter Three

1. Tom Collins, *Such Is Life*, in the "Sirius" edition (Sydney, 1962), Chap. I; pp. 40-42.
2. Henry Newbolt, Poems, *New and Old* (London, 1917), p. 67. Quoted by permission.
3. F. J. Child (ed.), *The English and Scottish Popular Ballads* (New York, 1962), Vol. IV, p. 143.
4. See, e.g., Alfred Buchanan, *The Real Australia* (London, 1907), pp. 133-35. The spelling was "Joyous Guard" in the First Edition.
5. *Reminiscences and Unpublished Poems* (Sydney and Melbourne, n.d.), Item #9.
6. Miss Edith Humphris quotes these lines with a slightly different arrangement, in her *Life*, p. 81. She suggests that they were "omitted" by Marcus Clarke. This seems misleading, since they do not appear in the edition of 1870.
7. *Advertiser*, March 23, 1912, p. 20.
8. Stockdale's penciled notes are preserved in the Mitchell Library, in Sydney.
9. *Register* (Adelaide), December 26, 1921, p. 2.
10. Francis W. L. Adams, *Australian Essays* (Melbourne and London, 1886), p. 21.
11. H. Northrop Frye, "La Tradition Narrative dans la Poésie Canadienne-Anglaise," *Gants du Ciel*, Spring, 1946.

Chapter Four

1. F. Klaeber (ed.), *Beowulf*, 3rd ed. (Boston, 1941), pp. 231, 235.
2. W. J. Alexander (ed.), *Shorter Poems* (Toronto, 1924), p. 121.
3. F. J. Child (ed.), *The English and Scottish Popular Ballads* (New York, 1962), Vol. IV, pp. 164-76.
4. For a sample of the unfavorable opinions of *Ashtaroth*, see A. J. Coombes, *Some Australian Poets* (Sydney and London, 1938), p. 45.

Chapter Five

1. Holograph letter in the Mitchell Library, Sydney, N.S.W.
2. Hugh McCrae, *My Father and My Father's Friends*, Intro. T. Inglis Moore (Sydney, 1935), p. 41.
3. The writer has heard him discuss this point in a lecture to a class of graduate students at Victoria College, Toronto.
4. Reprinted from Natural History Studies, in W. J. Alexander (ed.), *Short Stories and Essays* (Toronto, 1928).
5. Francis W. L. Adams, *Australian Essays* (Melbourne and London, 1886), p. 20.
6. Lord Charnwood, *Abraham Lincoln*, Chap. III, Section 3.

Chapter Six

1. See, e.g., H. L. Helson (ed.), *Theoretical Foundations of Psychology* (Princeton, 1951), p. 254; also Robinson and Robinson (eds.), *Readings in General Psychology* (Chicago, 1930), p. 591.
2. There was originally a further stanza of sixteen lines, canceled before publication. See the Robb edition (Oxford, 1962), p. 377. Gordon's judgment was surely right; the ending is much stronger as we have it.
3. In the 1960's they are more in tune with one aspect of the spirit of the times.
4. William Murdock, *Poems and Songs* (Saint John, 1860), p. 147.
5. There is no reason to doubt that Nolan, mentioned by name in Fytte VII of "Ye Wearie Wayfarer," is the prototype of the young hero in "The Roll of the Kettledrum."
6. Robert Browning, "La Saisiaz," line 359.
7. For a firsthand study of courage and fear in the lives of airline pilots, see E. K. Gann, *Fate Is the Hunter* (New York, 1961), esp. Chap. XV.
8. See above, p. 66.

Chapter Seven

1. Horace, *Odes*, Book I, Ode xv. Gordon has made a creditably faithful translation. For the benefit of anyone wishing to make a quick comparison, here is a prose translation of the first twelve lines:
   When the treacherous shepherd transported Helen, *his* hostess, across [through] the waves in ships *made of* Idaean *pine*, Nereus smothered the swift winds in an unwelcome quiet, that he might chant of evil fates. "According to an omen, you bring home *a load of* evils. What you take, Greece, sworn to destroy your marriage and the long-established reign of Priam, will seek to recover with a large army. Alas! What sweat there is for horses,

for men! What deaths of the Trojan race you are bringing to
pass! Now is Pallas preparing shield and helmet, and chariots,
and her anger."

2. The Preface to this edition by the Oxford University Press is
dated from Melbourne, April 20, 1912. The "First Australian
Edition" was issued in 1946, reprinted 1950, 1955, 1962. The
section here referred to comprises pp. lxxxiii-cxx.

3. See, e.g., J. P. Matthews, *Tradition in Exile* (1962), pp. 160-73;
and John Manifold, *Who Wrote the Ballads?* (Sydney, 1964),
passim.

4. Matthews, *op. cit.,* p. 171.

5. See D. Sladen, in the "Abbey Memorial Volume," p. 67.

Chapter Eight

1. Leonie Kramer has taken a long step in this direction, by her
article on "The Literary Reputation of Adam Lindsay Gordon,"
Australian Literary Studies (University of Tasmania), Vol. I,
No. I, June, 1963.

2. Cited as from "an unpublished essay," in Duncan Campbell
Scott's Introduction to the collected volume of Lampman's
poems, *Lyrics of Earth* (Toronto, 1925).

3. Edith Humphris and Douglas Sladen, *Adam Lindsay Gordon and
His Friends in England and Australia* (London, 1912), p. 254.

4. *Ibid.*

5. P. R. Stephensen, *The Foundations of Culture in Australia*
(Gordon, 1936), p. 29.

6. For this phrase and some others that follow, I stand indebted to
Professor T. Inglis Moore, of the Australian National University,
Canberra.

7. Tom Collins, *Such Is Life* (Sydney, 1961), p. vi.

8. Susanna Moodie, *Roughing It in the Bush* (London, 1852),
passim.

9. *Such Is Life,* p. 254.

10. Cf. John P. Matthews, *Tradition in Exile* (Toronto and Melbourne, 1962), pp. 22 f.

11. Donald Hankey, *A Student in Arms* (Toronto, 1917), p. 87.

12. William C. Wentworth, "Australasia," as in T. Inglis Moore
(ed.), *Poetry in Australia,* Vol. I, "From the Ballads to Brennan"
(Sydney, 1964).

13. This point is made in H. M. Green, *A History of Australian
Literature* (Sydney, 1961), Vol. I, p. 154.

14. Cf. Humphris and Sladen, *op. cit.,* p. 45; also D. Sladen, *Adam
Lindsay Gordon,* the "Westminster Abbey Memorial Volume"
(London, n.d.), p. 100.

15. *Saturday Evening Post,* July 25, 1953, p. 83.

16. *The Argus* (Melbourne), May 17, 1919, p. 5.

17. Cf. Chap. VI, above.

18. Matthews, *op. cit.*, p. 166.
19. Reprinted from *Tales of the Old Regime* (1897), in W. Murdoch and H. Drake-Brockman (ed.), *Australian Short Stories* (London, 1951).
20. Stephensen, *loc. cit.*
21. Humphris and Sladen, *op. cit.*, pp. 42 f.
22. In the more abstract and international art of musical performance, the claim is more generally allowed, as in the cases of Percy Grainger and Dame Nellie Melba.
23. The two-volume edition of Blair, Hornberger and Stewart, (eds.), *The Literature of the United States* (Chicago, 1947) gives fifty-six pages to James and ten to Eliot.
24. For an eminently sensible discussion of this topic, see H. M. Green, *op. cit.*, Vol. I, pp. xi-xiv.
25. The earliest publication of Gordon's poems in England, as listed in the Commonwealth National Library's bibliography, was in 1897, by Robert A. Thompson, in London.
26. Humphris and Sladen, *op. cit.*, p. 254.
27. Rev. J. J. Malone, *Gordon: The Australian Poet* (Melbourne, n.d., but cat. 1904), p. 3.
28. Holograph letter in the Mitchell Library. The letter is initialed on behalf of the firm, "A. W. M."
29. Francis W. L. Adams, *The Australians* (London, 1893), p. 10.
30. D. H. Rankin, *The Development and Philosophy of Australian Aestheticism* (Melbourne, 1949), p. 102.

Chapter Nine

1. See Leonie Kramer, "The Literary Reputation of Adam Lindsay Gordon," *Australian Literary Studies* (University of Tasmania), Vol. I, No. I, June, 1963, pp. 42-56.

Bibliography

Primary Sources

A. *Publication of Gordon's poems in his lifetime*
The Feud. A ballad dedicated to Noel Paton, R. S. A., as a key to his illustrations of "The Dowie Dens o' Yarrow," by A. Lindsay. Mount Gambier: Laurie, Watson and Laurie, 1864. (Reprinted, 1964, by Rigby, at Adelaide).
Ashtaroth; a dramatic lyric. By the author of "Sea Spray and Smoke Drift." Melbourne: Clarson, Massina, 1867.
Sea Spray and Smoke Drift. By the author of "Ashtaroth." Melbourne: George Robertson, 1867.
Bush Ballads and Galloping Rhymes. By the author of "Ashtaroth." Melbourne: Clarson, Massina, 1870.
B. *Texts and reference-material*
The earliest recorded collected edition was published in 1877, by Clarson, Massina. This was an omnibus volume with separate title pages for the three sections. Similar editions appeared, under the imprint of A. H. Massina, in 1878 and in 1880. The edition of 1880 contained the Preface by Marcus Clarke. Later editions, too numerous and too varied to be listed here, culminated in the Robb edition noted immediately below.
ROBB, FRANK MALDEN. Ed. *The Poems of Adam Lindsay Gordon* (1912). Melbourne, London, Wellington, New York: Oxford University Press, "First Australian edition," 1946· (Reprinted 1950, 1955, 1962). This is the available, and despite some faults still the best, collected edition.
Commonwealth National Library, *A Bibliography of Adam Lindsay Gordon.* Mimeographed; hence available to a limited extent only.
GORDON, ADAM LINDSAY. Holograph letters in the Mitchell Library, Sydney, and in the South Australian Library, Adelaide.
——————. "Hunting Under the Southern Cross," MS., in longhand, 25 pp., bound, in the Commonwealth National Library, Canberra.
——————. "MSS., Newspaper Cuttings, etc." 2 vols., in the Mitchell Library, Sydney.

──────. *Reminiscences and Unpublished Poems of Adam Lindsay Gordon.* Sydney and Melbourne: Somerset Publishing Co., n.d.

Land Titles Office, Adelaide. "Record of A. L. G.'s transactions in land," 5 pp., foolscap, typescript, in the South Australian Archives, Adelaide.

"Letter Book," of press-cuttings, holograph letters, typescript copies, programs, having to do with the unveiling of the Gordon bust in Westminster Abbey; in the Australian National Library, Canberra.

MATHER, JOHN BAXTER. "Adam Lindsay Gordon," newspaper cuttings from the *Border Watch*, 1931. Volume in the Public Library of South Australia, Adelaide.

MOIR, J. K. "Adam Lindsay Gordon," bound volume of typescript, with photo-prints mounted. 575 pp., quarto. In the Melbourne Public Library, with carbon copies elsewhere. This is a most useful collection of material, containing an elaborate chronology of Gordon's life.

"Newscuttings," Vol. 165, in the Mitchell Library, Sydney.

"Press Contributions," V, in the Mitchell Library, Sydney.

"Research Notes," in the South Australian Archives. #28, on the wreck of the *Admella;* #30, on Gordon's career in the South Australian Police Force.

SERLE, PERCIVAL. *A Bibliography of Australian Poetry and Verse.* Melbourne University Press, 1925.

──────. *Dictionary of Australian Biography.* Sydney and London: Angus & Robertson, 1949.

South Australian Archives. Correspondence between T. P. E. Warburton and G. B. Scott, 1855, relative to Gordon's resignation from the Police Force.

Secondary Sources

Books

ADAMS, FRANCIS W. L. *Australian Essays.* Melbourne: William Inglis & Co., and London: Griffith, Farran & Co., 1886.

──────. *The Australians.* London: T. Fisher Unwin, 1893. These two books by Adams are unusually perceptive, and throw light on the Victorian period in Australian thought and letters.

BYRNE, DESMOND. *Australian Writers.* London: Rich. Bentley & Son, 1896.

COOMBES, A. J. *Some Australian Poets.* Sydney and London: Angus & Robertson, 1938. Contains an exemplary account of Gordon's life, lucid and well organized.

FETHERSTONHAUGH, CUTHBERT. *After Many Days.* Melbourne, Sydney

152 ADAM LINDSAY GORDON

and Adelaide: E. W. Cole, Book Arcade, n.d. (Preface dated
November, 1917). A volume of reminiscences, with ten pages
given to Gordon.

GRATTAN, C. HARTLEY. *Introducing Australia.* New York: The John
Day Co., 1942. A readable introduction to things Australian.

————. Ed. *Australia.* Berkeley and Los Angeles: University of Cali-
fornia Press, 1947.

GREEN, H. M. *Fourteen Minutes.* Sydney and London: Angus &
Robertson, 1944. A book of "talks," one being on Gordon.

————. *A History of Australian Literature.* 2 vols. Sydney: Angus &
Robertson, 1961.

HADGRAFT, CECIL. *Australian Literature.* London, Melbourne and
Toronto: Heinemann, 1960.

HOARE, BENJAMIN. *Looking Gaily Back.* Melbourne: E. W. Cole,
Book Arcade, 1927.

HUMPHRIS, EDITH. *The Life of Adam Lindsay Gordon.* London: Eric
Partridge Ltd., n.d. (Evidently written in 1933, and published
in 1935. See the *Australian Encyclopaedia,* 1963, Vol. IV, p.
338.)

————— and Sladen, Douglas. *Adam Lindsay Gordon and His Friends
in England and Australia.* London: Constable & Co., 1912. An
omnium gatherum of biography, anecdote, legend, reminiscences,
and source material, profusely illustrated. Not wholly depend-
able, but an indispensable tool for a knowledge of Gordon's life
and times.

McCRAE, HUGH. *My Father and My Father's Friends.* Intro. T. Inglis
Moore. Sydney: Angus & Robertson, 1935.

MALONE, REV. J. J. *Gordon: The Australian Poet.* Melbourne: The
Australian Catholic Truth Society, n.d. (Catalogued, 1904).

MANIFOLD, JOHN S. *Who Wrote the Ballads?* Sydney: Australasian
Book Society, 1964.

MATTHEWS, JOHN P. *Tradition in Exile.* Toronto: University of Toronto
Press, in association with F. W. Cheshire, Melbourne, 1962.

MILLER, E. MORRIS. *Australian Literature.* 2 vols. Melbourne University Press, 1940. A rich mine of information, though the critical
judgments are capricious.

————. *Idem.* Revised by F. T. Macartney. Sydney: Angus & Robertson, 1956. This revision is arranged encyclopaedia-fashion, alpha-
betically by authors. It is more concise than the original version,
but more convenient for quick reference.

MOSSMAN, SAMUEL. *Narrative of the Shipwreck of the "Admella."*
Melbourne: J. H. Moulines & Co., 1859. A detailed account of
the event from which Gordon's "From the Wreck" is almost certainly derived.

O'LEARY, P. I. *Bard in Bondage.* Melbourne: Hawthorne Press, 1954.

O'NEILL, REV. GEORGE. *Life of the Reverend Julian Edmund Tenison
Woods.* Sydney, Melbourne, Brisbane: Pellegrini & Co., 1929.

PALMER, E. VANCE. Ed. *A. G. Stephens. His Life and Work.* Melbourne: Robertson & Mullens, 1941.

RANKIN, D. H. *The Development and Philosophy of Australian Aestheticism.* Melbourne: J. Roy Stevens, 1949. A somewhat old-fashioned treatise, with several references to Gordon and his place in the development of an Australian ethos.

ROSS, J. HOWLETT. *The Laureate of the Centaurs. A Memoir of the Life of Adam Lindsay Gordon with New Poems, Prose Sketches, Political Speeches, and Reminiscences, and an "In Memoriam"* by Kendall. London: Samuel J. Mullen, 1888.

SAMUEL, H. J., and HEDDLE, ENID M. *Boy on a Horse. The Story of Adam Lindsay Gordon.* Melbourne: F. W. Cheshire, 1957. Also, London and New Zealand: Angus & Robertson. A work of biographical fiction.

SLADEN, DOUGLAS. *Adam Lindsay Gordon: The Life and Best Poems of the Poet of Australia.* The Westminster Abbey Memorial Volume. London: Hutchinson & Co., n.d.

STEPHENS, W. J. *South Australia. Its Wealth and Beauty.* Bendigo: Cambridge Press, 1939. "Memories of Gordon" take up eleven pages.

STEPHENSEN, P. R. *The Foundations of Culture in Australia.* Gordon: W. J. Miles, 1936. Mainly hostile to Gordon.

SUTHERLAND, ALEXANDER. *Victoria and its Metropolis.* 2 vols. Melbourne: McCarron, Bird & Co., 1888.

TURNER, H. G. and SUTHERLAND, ALEXANDER. *The Development of Australian Literature.* Melbourne, Sydney, Adelaide, Brisbane and London: George Robertson & Co., 1898. An early and lively, but unreliable, account of Gordon.

VAUGHAN, CRAWFORD. *Golden Wattle Time.* ("The Dramatic Story of Adam Lindsay Gordon.") Sydney: Frank Johnson, 1942.

VIDLER, EDWARD A. Ed. *The Adam Lindsay Gordon Memorial Volume.* Melbourne and Sydney: The Lothian Publishing Co. Pty. Ltd., 1926.

Articles in Periodicals

ANON. "Adam Lindsay Gordon," *Lone Hand,* October 1, 1912.

————. "At Gordon's Grave," *Argus,* June 27, 1892.

————. "A Reminiscence of Adam Lindsay Gordon," *Adelaide Observer,* July 1, 1899.

A. S. "Adam Lindsay Gordon, Australian Poet," *Once A Week,* II, iv (April 15, 1885), 241-47.

"Adam Lindsay Gordon—English Opinions," *All About Books,* VI, vii (July 12, 1934). 136-37.

ADAMS, FRANCIS W. L. "Australian Criticism and the Reaction against Gordon," *Centennial Magazine,* II, vii (February, 1890), 547-52.

BINNS, KENNETH. Letter to the Editor of the *Argus*, November 28, 1923. Concerns the order of publication of Gordon's first two volumes, in 1867.

BRAZENOR, WILLIAM. "Gordon in Ballarat," *Argus*, October 11, 1913.

CHAPMAN, A. L. "Adam Lindsay Gordon," *Sydney Quarterly Magazine*, IX, ii (June, 1892), 125-30.

COLE, P. R. "The Poetry of Gordon," *Leisure Hour*, I, vii (April 15, 1927), 6-8, 35-37.

HAMMERSLEY, J. "Personal Reminiscences of Adam Lindsay Gordon," *Victorian Review*, X (May, 1884), 66-69.

HERVEY, G. "Adam Lindsay Gordon Guff," *Truth*, November, 1912.

HOLDSWORTH, P. J. "Adam Lindsay Gordon. A Brief Sketch," *Illustrated Sydney News*, XXVI, v (May 2, 1889), 9, 28.

HUMPHRIS, EDITH. "The Youth of Adam Lindsay Gordon," *Lone Hand*, VII, xl (August 1, 1910), 265-73

ILBURY, MR. and MRS. T. H. "Adam Lindsay Gordon: His Connection with Western Australia," *Western Australian Historical Society Journal and Proceedings*, I, ii (1928), 56-60.

KAYE, EILEEN. "Adam Lindsay Gordon. A Biography," *Australasian*, in installments from August 19, 1933, to December 23, 1933. An excellent account of Gordon's life.

KRAMER, LEONIE. "The Literary Reputation of Adam Lindsay Gordon," *Australian Literary Studies*, I, i (June, 1963), 42-56. This article may well mark the beginning of a new era in Gordon studies.

LAUDER, MRS. ELIZABETH ANNIE (*née* Bright). *Reminiscences, Melbourne Record*, June 25, 1910.

LONG, C. R. "Gordon—Poet and Sportsman," *The Australian Quarterly*, No. 20 (December 14, 1933), pp. 82-88.

LOW, MARGARET (Mrs. Peter). Interview "By our Special Reporter," *The Advertiser* (Adelaide), March 23, 1912.

LOW, W. PARK. "Gordon and Miss Park," letter to the editor of *The Chronicle* (Adelaide), May 14, 1932.

McCRAE, GEORGE GORDON. "Adam Lindsay Gordon," *Southerly*, V, i (1944), 26-28.

MARTIN, ARTHUR PATCHETT. "Two Australian Poets," *Melbourne Review*, V (January-October 1880), 443-51.

S. S. T. "Australian Poetry," *Melbourne Review*, I (January-October, 1876), 202-30.

SAUNDERS, A. T. "Adam Lindsay Gordon and the Admella's Wreck," *The Register* (Adelaide), December 28, 1921.

SIMON, H. C. "Adam Lindsay Gordon. The Politician," *The Register* (Adelaide), May 24, 1926.

SOWARD, G. K. "In Adam Lindsay Gordon's Country," *Lone Hand*, January 1, 1910, 547-48.

STOCKDALE, HARRY. "Adam Lindsay Gordon. Interesting Reminiscences," *The Argus*, May 17, 1919, p. 5.

SUTHERLAND, ALEXANDER. "Adam Lindsay Gordon. A Memoir," *The Melbourne Review*, VIII (January-October, 1883), 424-47.
WOODS, JULIAN E. TENISON. "Personal Reminiscences of Adam Lindsay Gordon," *Melbourne Review*, IX (January-October, 1884), 131-41.

Index